# Ready, Set, Go... Get Granted

## A Nonprofit Grant Writing Workbook

*FIRST EDITION*

*DR. HEIDI GREGORY-MINA*

*Ready, Set, Go...Get Granted*
*A Grant Writing Workbook*

*DR. HEIDI - The Book Publisher © 2023*



*ISBN: 979-8-218-28059-8*

# Dedication

*This book is dedicated to my parents, who have always stood by me and been my greatest supporters. Throughout my journey, they have been a constant source of love, encouragement, and belief in my abilities. Their unwavering support has shaped me into the person I am today.*

*To my parents, thank you for instilling in me the values of perseverance, determination, and resilience. Your guidance and wisdom have given me the strength to overcome challenges and pursue my dreams fearlessly.*

*I am grateful for the sacrifices you have made to provide me with opportunities and a nurturing environment. Your unwavering faith in my abilities has inspired me to strive for excellence and reach for the stars.*

*You have been my pillars of strength, offering guidance, reassurance, and unconditional love at every step of my journey. Your belief in me has fueled my ambitions and empowered me to pursue my passions wholeheartedly.*

*This book is a tribute to your unwavering support and a token of my deep appreciation for everything you have done for me. I am forever grateful for your love, sacrifices, and constant presence in my life.*

*With all my love and gratitude,*

**Heidi**

# Table Of Contents

# How to use this Workbook

The grant book/workbook is a helpful resource designed to assist you in navigating the grant application process and managing your grant-funded project effectively. To make the most of the grant book/workbook, here are some suggestions on how to use it:

1. **Find a quiet and comfortable space**: Choose a dedicated workspace where you can concentrate on the grant book/workbook without distractions. This will allow you to focus on the tasks at hand.
2. **Gather the necessary materials**: Have a pen or pencil, and if you prefer, a notebook or blank sheets of paper ready. These materials will enable you to write down important notes, ideas, and action items as you work through the grant book/workbook.
3. **Read the instructions**: Take the time to thoroughly read the instructions provided for each section or exercise in the grant book/workbook. Understanding the purpose and objective of each task will help you approach it effectively.
4. **Reflect and brainstorm**: When prompted, reflect on the questions or prompts given in the grant book/workbook. Consider the specific requirements of the grant application or the needs of your project. Use your pen and paper or the designated spaces in the workbook to jot down your thoughts, ideas, and relevant information.
5. **Be thorough and organized**: As you work through the grant book/workbook, strive to be comprehensive and organized in your responses. Provide clear and concise information, and ensure that you address all relevant aspects related to the grant application or project management.
6. **Take your time**: Grant applications and project management require careful thought and planning. Avoid rushing through the grant book/workbook exercises. Take the time to consider each question and task carefully, allowing yourself to develop well-thought-out and compelling responses.
7. **Review and revise**: Once you have completed a section or exercise, review your answers. Check for any errors, inconsistencies, or areas that require further clarification. Revise your responses as needed to ensure accuracy and coherence.
8. **Track your progress**: As you work through the grant book/workbook, keep track of your progress. Note any milestones achieved, deadlines met, or tasks completed. This will help you stay organized and motivated throughout the grant application process and project implementation.
9. **Revisit and update**: The grant book/workbook can serve as a valuable resource even after the initial grant application is submitted. Revisit the book/workbook periodically to update information, document progress, and address any changes or challenges that arise during the project lifecycle.

Remember, the grant book/workbook is designed to guide you through the grant application process and support effective project management. By using pen and paper or a notebook along side the workbook, you can further capture and organize your thoughts, making the experience more interactive and personalized. Utilize the grant book/workbook as a tool to structure your thinking, document essential information, and enhance your chances of success in securing and managing grant funding.

# Preface

The complexity of grant writing can be overwhelming for most individuals. When I started in the grant management field, terms like indirect costs, direct costs, fringe benefit rates, NOGA, PAR, etc., left me utterly lost. It felt like I had stumbled into an alternate universe! However, after about three years, I began to feel more comfortable with some grant-making mechanisms, and at about five years in, I felt like an expert. Despite this, I continue to learn new things as the field constantly changes and evolves, which makes it both exciting and challenging. With a vast amount of grant-making agencies and little streamlining, there is much room for continuous learning. While it can be frustrating at times, the payoffs can be highly motivating. In a sense, the grant management field is like a "bet the company" type of field.

When I consult with non-profit agencies that are new to grant writing, they are often surprised by the amount of work that goes into a successful application. Before beginning to write a grant, the most critical step is ensuring that you have collected data to defend your nonprofit's work and impact. However, many nonprofits have not thought to collect the necessary data or collect it in the correct format. Some data we should be collected to help support grant applications include:

Program data: This includes data on the number of people served, the types of services provided, and the impact of those services on the community. For example, a nonprofit that provides job training services should collect data on the number of people who have completed the program, the types of jobs they have secured, and their income levels before and after the training.

Financial data: This includes information on the nonprofit's budget, expenses, and revenue sources. Nonprofits should be prepared to provide detailed financial statements, including balance sheets, income statements, and cash flow statements.

Demographic data: This includes information on the population served by the nonprofit, including age, gender, race, and income level. Nonprofits should collect data on the demographics of their clients to demonstrate the need for their services and the impact they are having on the community.

Impact data: This includes data on the outcomes and impact of the nonprofit's programs and services. Nonprofits should collect data on the short-term and long-term impact of their work, including changes in behavior, attitudes, and knowledge among their clients.

Organizational data: This includes information on the nonprofit's history, mission, and governance structure. Nonprofits should be prepared to provide a detailed description of their organization, including their mission statement, board of directors, and key staff members.

Therefore, we typically spend the first six months identifying the needed data and creating a data collection plan.

Once we have the necessary data, we can move forward to the grant application writing.

However, searching for and locating funding opportunities can be time-consuming. It can take anywhere from a few weeks to several months to find a good match, and sometimes even longer. I advise nonprofits to make this a regular part of their internal tasks, even though it can be frustrating to find a good match. Taking the time to find a suitable funding opportunity initially can save time and resources in the long run.

One of the biggest mistakes non-profit organizations make is falling victim to mission creep. Mission creep is the gradual and unintended shift in an organization's mission or focus over time, often due to pursuing funding opportunities or other external pressures. When nonprofits stray too far from their core mission or purpose, it can dilute their impact and effectiveness, and may result in losing support from their stakeholders. When eager to find a grant, they may apply for opportunities that are not aligned with their mission, which results in a rejected application. Such a misaligned application can use up valuable time and resources. However, with more research, non-profits can find a good match and focus their efforts and resources on a funding opportunity with a higher likelihood of being funded.

Hiring a consultant to train staff members on grant writing best practices can be a cost-effective way for smaller non-profits to build their internal capacity for grant writing. By investing in the training of current staff, the organization can become more self-sufficient in the long run and avoid the need to continually hire outside consultants for grant writing services. Additionally, having trained staff can lead to a more comprehensive and accurate application process, as they will have a better understanding of the non-profit's needs and goals. This approach can be a valuable investment in the future success of the non-profit and help them secure the funding needed to achieve their mission.

However, even hiring a consultant for training may be too expensive for some smaller non-profits. In such cases, they can consider reaching out to a local university with a Master's in Nonprofit program. These programs often have students who are eager to gain hands-on experience working with non-profit organizations. As part of their coursework, they may be required to work on a project for a non-profit organization, which can include grant writing. This can be a great opportunity for non-profits to get the help they need at little to no cost, while also providing students with valuable real-world experience.

If your non-profit has never applied for a grant before, I highly recommend starting small. Post-award management of a grant requires a lot of work, and funders want assurance that their funds will be well-managed. Without a track record, it is riskier for a funder to invest in your non-profit. In a highly competitive environment, funders may choose the less risky option. According to a 2019 survey by the Center for Effective Philanthropy, grantmakers reported that they received an average of 167 proposals for every 10 grants awarded, indicating a highly competitive environment for grant funding. Additionally, the same survey found that only 41% of grant applicants received the full amount of funding requested, further highlighting the importance of starting small and building a track record of successful grant management (Smith, 2021).

Collaborating with a larger organization can provide several benefits to a smaller non-profit seeking to build up its grant writing capacity. By partnering with an established organization, the smaller non-profit can leverage the larger organization's expertise and resources to successfully manage grants and community relationships. Additionally, the collaborative effort can demonstrate to funders that the smaller non-profit has the capacity to work effectively with others towards a common goal. This can increase the non-profit's credibility and likelihood of securing future grants. Furthermore, funders often look favorably on collaborative efforts as they can achieve greater impact and reach a wider audience. According to a study conducted by the Bridgespan Group, 75% of funders prefer collaborative funding models, such as partnerships and joint ventures, to individual nonprofits (Neeley, 2018). Overall, partnering with a larger organization can be a strategic and effective way for a smaller non-profit to build up its grant writing capacity and increase its chances of success in securing funding.

For example, a small non-profit focused on providing education and job training for low-income youth could partner with a larger organization with expertise in workforce development. Together, they could apply for a grant to expand their program and provide additional resources and opportunities to more youth in the community. The larger organization could provide support in grant management and community relationships, while the smaller non-profit could contribute their knowledge and expertise in working with the specific population they serve. This collaborative effort would allow both organizations to achieve greater impact and leverage their resources to make a significant difference in the community. Funders would likely be impressed by this joint effort and see the potential for long-term success in addressing the issue of youth unemployment and underemployment.

Starting small can provide your non-profit with a valuable learning experience that can help build up its grant writing skills and capacity. When you begin with smaller grants, you can focus on developing and improving your grant writing process, including collecting and organizing data, identifying relevant funding opportunities, and building relationships with funders. As you gain more experience and successfully manage smaller grants, your non-profit can build its reputation and credibility in the grant writing world, which can ultimately lead to more significant funding opportunities in the future. Moreover, starting small can help your organization become more efficient and effective in managing grants, and you can apply the skills and knowledge you gain from smaller grants to more significant and complex grant applications. By building up your grant writing capacity over time, your non-profit can increase its chances of success in future grant applications and secure the funding it needs to achieve its mission.

Demonstrating the ability to effectively manage smaller grants is a critical step towards building your non-profit's track record and reputation. Successfully managing these grants helps your organization build trust and demonstrate accountability, which are essential factors for funders when considering grant applications. By proving your organization's capability to deliver on its promises and manage resources responsibly, funders may be more likely to consider awarding larger grants in the future. This not only helps your non-profit achieve its mission but also establishes long-term partnerships with funders who can support your organization's growth and impact over time. Ultimately, building a successful track record takes time, but starting with smaller grants and consistently demonstrating your organization's capacity for effective management can help your non-profit establish itself as a reliable and trustworthy recipient of larger grants.

Moreover, starting small can also help you identify and address any gaps in your organization's capacity or resources. By managing smaller grants, you can identify areas where your non-profit needs to improve and take steps to address them before pursuing larger funding opportunities. This can help ensure that your non-profit is better positioned for success in the long run. Partnering with a larger organization can also provide additional resources and support for your non-profit, allowing you to take on more ambitious projects and expand your impact. This type of collaboration can also help build relationships within the non-profit community and potentially lead to future funding opportunities.

One of the biggest challenges of grant writing is navigating the different requirements and expectations of funders. Each funder has their own priorities, preferences, and specific application guidelines. While this can be overwhelming, it also presents an opportunity for growth and development. As a grant writer, you can continuously expand your skills and knowledge to meet the various demands of different funders. With each application, you gain valuable experience and insights that you can apply to future proposals.

In addition to the challenges posed by different funders, grant writers also face the task of repetition. It can be tempting to copy and paste sections of a previous grant into a new application, especially if the information seems relevant. However, each grant should be treated as a standalone document. Reviewers may jump around when reviewing an application, and it is essential to ensure that each section provides a complete picture of your organization's work and impact. Therefore, grant writers should strive to write each section with clarity and precision, avoiding the temptation to rely on previous work.

Grants.gov is a great resource for nonprofits applying for federal grants, as it streamlines the submission process and provides consistency across all federal grant applications. However, it's important to note that the majority of nonprofits apply for grants from foundations and corporations, which often have different requirements and application processes. Despite these differences, there are some commonalities that can be found among all grant applications.

For example, all funders want to see a clear and compelling narrative that explains the nonprofit's mission, goals, and how the grant will help achieve those goals. They want to know the specific activities and outcomes that will result from the grant funding, and how the nonprofit will measure success. Additionally, all funders want to see a well-planned budget that aligns with the proposed activities and outcomes, and a strong understanding of the nonprofit's capacity to successfully manage and execute the proposed project.

By focusing on these commonalities, nonprofits can develop a strong grant application regardless of the type of funder they are applying to. It's important to thoroughly research each funder's specific requirements and tailor the application accordingly, but by keeping these underlying commonalities in mind, nonprofits can create a strong and compelling case for funding.

## TYPES OF GRANTS

Grants can be categorized into three main categories: Federal and State agencies, Private Foundations and Organizations, and Corporate Grants. Government grants are made available by federal and state agencies through legislative appropriations. Grants.gov (www.grants.gov) offers a one-stop platform for most federal grants. Table one provides a list of federal grant-making agencies that post their requests for proposals (RFP) on Grants.gov.

Table 1. Federal Grant-Making Agencies Using Grants.gov

**Federal Grant-Making Agencies**

Department of Agriculture
Department of Commerce
Department of Defense Department of Education
Department of Energy Federal Emergency
Department of Health and Human Services
Department of Housing and Urban Development
Department of the Interior
Department of Justice
Department of Labor
Department of State
Department of Transportation
Department of the Treasury

Department of Veterans Affairs
Agency for International Development
Corporation for National Service

Environmental Protection Agency
Federal Emergency Management Agency
Institute for Museum and Library Services
National Aeronautical and Space Admin
National Archives and Records Admin
National Endowment for the Arts
National Endowment for the Humanities
National Science Foundation
Small Business Administration
Social Security Administration

Private grants generally come from foundations, private organizations, and businesses. There are over 119,000 foundations and private grant-making organizations in the United States. Each foundation or private organization has its own application process, leading to many opportunities and just as many challenges. There is minor streamlining or consolidation of the grant application process with these funders. The most commonly used website for searching for foundation grants is The Foundation Center (www.fconline.fdncenter.org). However, a good google search using keywords will also reveal many grant-making agencies in different subject areas. Additionally, your geographic region should be searched. This is commonly overlooked. Some funders will fund in any subject area as long as it is within a specific region or serving a particular population.

The third major grant-making category is corporate grants. Businesses make corporate grants available that serve the general community, for example, banks that offer grants to enhance the local community. This also helps organizations fulfill the pressure they face from stakeholders and consumers to be socially responsible. You will easily find links to corporate foundations of certain corporations. When searching, you will want to target corporations that work in the area where you are providing your programs and services. For example, if you are an animal rescue, you would look at the Petco and PetSmart Foundation. Typically, corporate foundations will provide grants in their business sector.

## TYPES OF GRANTS INSTRUMENTS

There are many different types of grant instruments, which can confuse the new grant writer. Grant instruments can include a wide range of funding mechanisms such as contracts, cooperative agreements, fellowships, loans, and grants-in-aid, and understanding the nuances of each is critical to crafting a successful grant proposal (Sridharan & Li, 2016). Below is a list of the instruments with their definitions:

- **Gift** - Usually no strings are attached to this, not for a specific project. It is tax-deductible for the donor.
- **Grant** – Given to carry out basic research with particular deliverables and time frames for the work.
- **Contract** – An agreement between two parties; the Sponsor will provide funding, and the Recipient (Contractor) will provide services or deliver a product.
- **Cooperative Agreement** - An award of financial assistance that is similar to a grant but carries provisions for substantial involvement by the Sponsor in completing the proposed activity

The most significant discrepancy I have witnessed in my experience working with grants is the misuse of the terminology grant. Some organizations will provide funding for a specific purpose, such as a new roof on a barn, travel support for students to a conference, money to publish a children's book for children with autism, and so much more. While these are all great causes, they are donations or gifts with a specific purpose. They are simple applications with no required reporting or follow-up. A grant will require research and evaluation of a program or service and have post-award requirements. An example of this could be a program that provides inner-city children with after-school activities to keep them out of trouble. They would know if this program is successful if the rate of children getting in trouble decreases. The key is having an evaluation component to demonstrate the success of the program or service. Although these grants can be for only one year, they typically span three to five years.

## OVERVIEW OF THE GRANT WRITING PROCESS

The grant writing process refers to the activities involved in preparing a grant proposal for submission, which includes the pre-award stage of grants from identifying an opportunity to the submission of the proposal until the awarding of the grant. The following diagram lays out the pre-award grant process:

Once a non-profit organization is awarded a grant, it enters the post-award management phase, which involves implementing the proposed project, managing the budget, submitting progress

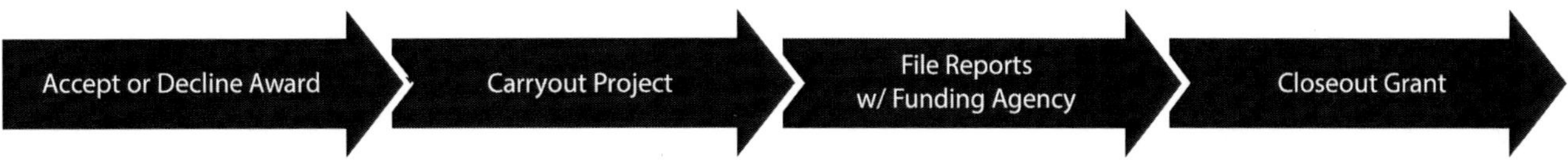


The time it takes to manage a grant is easily underestimated or often not considered. Each expense must be carefully considered, appropriately allocated, and diligently reported to the funder. Many funders require yearly or semi-annual reporting; however, this can be as frequent as monthly reporting. Therefore understanding the requirements before a grant application submission is critical to ensure your nonprofit has the resources to fulfill the obligations, or the necessary grant management resources have been accounted for within the grant application. Some best practices to follow are:

- **Create a grant management plan**: A grant management plan should outline the roles and responsibilities of all team members involved in managing the grant, the timeline for reporting requirements, and how the grant funds will be used. It should also include a budget plan with a breakdown of expenses and timelines for each expense.
- **Keep detailed records**: Keep accurate records of all grant-related expenses, including invoices, receipts, and payment records. These records will be necessary for reporting and auditing purposes.
- **Monitor grant progress**: Monitor grant progress to ensure that project milestones are being met and that funds are being spent appropriately. If there are any issues or changes to the project, communicate with the funder as soon as possible.
- **Submit reports on time**: Submit all required reports on time and in the format requested by the funder. Late or incomplete reports can harm the relationship with the funder and jeopardize future funding opportunities.
- **Communicate with the funder**: Maintain open lines of communication with the funder throughout the grant period. Keep them informed of any issues or successes related to the project, and be proactive in addressing any concerns they may have.
- **Conduct regular internal audits**: Conduct regular internal audits to ensure that all grant-related expenses are being tracked and reported accurately. This will also help identify any potential issues early on, allowing for corrective action to be taken before the funder becomes aware of any problems.

By following these best practices, non-profit organizations can ensure that they are effectively managing their grants, meeting reporting requirements, and maintaining positive relationships with funders. As we progress through this book, we will look at the different aspects of the grant writing process and post-award management of a grant.

# CHAPTER ONE
# Assessing Organizational Readiness and Searching for a Grant

Grants are a great way to expand a nonprofit's financial portfolio. While it is essential to diversify funding streams, you also need to be ready to take it on. The first step is getting your Board to back up this strategic addition. Once that is in place, readiness can be accessed. First, do you have at least six months of data to show that your program or service has successfully reached its goals? This data will vary depending on the type of program or service your nonprofit offers. For example, if your nonprofit focuses on helping at-risk seniors get into college, there are many data points your nonprofit needs to track. First, your nonprofit needs to define the population that will be/is served and what is considered at risk. In the context of high school seniors, an "at-risk population" generally refers to students who may face barriers or challenges that put them at a higher risk of not graduating on time or at all. This can include factors such as low academic achievement, low socioeconomic status, limited access to educational resources, English language learner status, or involvement in the juvenile justice system. Identifying and providing support to at-risk populations is an important aspect of ensuring that all students have the opportunity to succeed and reach their full potential.

Second, your nonprofit needs to track one group of high-school seniors they will be serving and another group they are not serving. The latter group will be your control group. A control group in research refers to a group of participants who are similar to the experimental group in all aspects except for the variable that is being tested. The purpose of a control group is to provide a baseline against which the results of the experimental group can be compared. Throughout the school year, the program will collect data on attendance, exam, project, and assignment grades. This can be compared to the previous year's work and the grades from the control group. Lastly, acceptance rates into college will demonstrate the impact of your program. If your nonprofit has programs and services but does not have this level of data collection, this needs to be the first step toward getting grants ready.

Then you also need to think about your post-award management. So often, we are excited by the prospect of funding that we do not think through the necessary resources. There is going to be ongoing reporting as well as post-award financial management. When I refer to management, I refer to payroll allocations, expense posting, approvals, purchasing supplies, tracking of data, etc. Additionally, your grant should have Institutional Review Board (IRB) approval if the program or service involves human subjects. IRB approval will assure the funder that quality assurance and protections are in place. If your organization does not have an internal review board (IRB) for research, you should first check whether your organization is legally required to have one. Depending on the type of research and the location of the organization, there may be laws or regulations that mandate the establishment of an IRB. Assuming there is no legal requirement, you may want to consider establishing an IRB within your organization to ensure that research is conducted in an ethical and responsible manner. Some possible steps to take include:

- Identify key stakeholders who would be involved in establishing an IRB, such as senior leadership, legal counsel, and research staff.
- Develop policies and procedures for the IRB, such as guidelines for research proposal submission,

review and approval processes, and monitoring and reporting requirements.

- Identify and train potential IRB members, who should be diverse in terms of expertise, experience, and backgrounds.
- Develop a system for monitoring and reporting research activities to ensure that approved protocols are being followed and any issues or concerns are promptly addressed.
- Establish a process for regular review and evaluation of the IRB's policies and procedures to ensure that they remain up-to-date and effective.

It's important to note that establishing an IRB requires significant time, resources, and expertise. If your organization is unable to do so, you may need to seek external review from an accredited IRB.

Lastly, do you have someone to write and edit grant applications and reports? These should be different individuals. Editing and writing are skills that take time to perfect. While you can hire someone to write the grant proposal for you, this does not help the nonprofit in the long term. Instead, a nonprofit should invest in professional development and training. We also need to remember that we must have someone conducting research and spending time searching for grants.

## SEARCHING FOR A GRANT

Once sufficient supporting data is available, the next step is finding a grant that aligns with your organization's mission through conducting a grant search. While that sounds easy enough, it can be challenging and time-consuming. However, finding a good match is critical to ensure mission creep does not happen. When your nonprofit decides to add grants to its portfolio, it is best to consistently keep looking for grant opportunities so there is always something in the pipeline. Having grant opportunities in the pipeline will prevent having to operate under stress to find funding under time pressures and deadlines, and waste time applying for the wrong grants. When you begin searching for a grant, you need to determine a couple of items prior. The following questions will guide you through this:

1. **WHICH PROGRAM OR SERVICE WILL YOU BE WRITING THE GRANT FOR?**

   ________________________________________

2. **WHAT WILL THE PURPOSE OF THE GRANT MONEY BE?**

   ________________________________________

3. **HOW MUCH MONEY DO YOU NEED TO ACHIEVE THE PURPOSE?**

   ________________________________________

While these three questions may seem straightforward and obvious, I have worked with many nonprofits that had not considered these questions and their importance. Many funders will not provide grants for general administrative use. A strategy needs to be developed around the programs or services you offer and for which ones you want to pursue funding. Once this is determined, then the purpose can be narrowed down. Is this for the expansion of a program or service? Is this for starting a new program or service based on a current successful program? Is this for moving a program or service into a new region? Creating a budget early on is a critical step that many nonprofits miss. Not taking the time to do to put together a proper budget can be costly later on. It will also help ensure the potential funder is offering funds in a range that will work for your program or service.

Additionally, it will ensure that you have thought through all the expenses and whether or not these will all be allowable on the direct costs of the grant. If these expenses are encountered after the grant is funded, it could cost your nonprofit money that was not budgeted. For example, many funders will not pay 100% of the cost of a laptop. They expect the expense to be shared as the usage will most likely exceed the program's scope or service. There may not be any money in the budget to absorb this cost share. A proper budget early on will expose and avoid such potential surprise costs.

So now that you have answered these questions, you want to think about possible grant funding organizations and the type of grants you wish to apply for. Before you begin searching, define some key words or funders you can research. As you develop your list, think about your program or service, the geographic region you service, the population you address, and so on. Take a few moments to create a list of search terms below:

| | | |
|---|---|---|
| ____________ | ____________ | ____________ |
| ____________ | ____________ | ____________ |
| ____________ | ____________ | ____________ |
| ____________ | ____________ | ____________ |
| ____________ | ____________ | ____________ |
| ____________ | ____________ | ____________ |
| ____________ | ____________ | ____________ |

Using these search terms, you can begin your Internet search. As you review different possibilities, remember to look at the dollar amounts they provide, ensure the deadline is reasonable, make sure your program or services mission aligns with the funder, and check any additional policies required by your Board are met. Select two or three funding possibilities for your organization and fill in the data below:

**POSSIBILITY NUMBER ONE:**

NAME OF FUNDER: ________________________________

TYPE OF FUNDER: ________________________________

THE MISSION OF FUNDER: ________________________________

HOW DOES YOUR PROJECT FIT WITH THE FUNDING AGENCY'S GOALS AND OBJECTIVES? (Expand beyond a yes or no)________________________________

________________________________

THE AMOUNT THEY WILL FUND: ________________________________

DEADLINE: ________________________________

ARE YOU ELIGIBLE? ________________________________

DO THEY COVER INDIRECT COSTS? ___

DO THEY REQUIRE COST SHARING? ___

**POSSIBILITY NUMBER TWO:**

NAME OF FUNDER: ___

TYPE OF FUNDER: ___

THE MISSION OF FUNDER: ___

HOW DOES YOUR PROJECT FIT WITH THE FUNDING AGENCY'S GOALS AND OBJECTIVES? (Expand beyond a yes or no)___

___

THE AMOUNT THEY WILL FUND: ___

DEADLINE: ___

ARE YOU ELIGIBLE? ___

DO THEY COVER INDIRECT COSTS? ___

DO THEY REQUIRE COST SHARING? ___

**POSSIBILITY NUMBER THREE:**

NAME OF FUNDER: ___

TYPE OF FUNDER: ___

THE MISSION OF FUNDER: ___

HOW DOES YOUR PROJECT FIT WITH THE FUNDING AGENCY'S GOALS AND OBJECTIVES? (Expand beyond a yes or no)___

___

THE AMOUNT THEY WILL FUND: ___

DEADLINE: ___

ARE YOU ELIGIBLE? ______________________________________________

DO THEY COVER INDIRECT COSTS? ___________________________________

DO THEY REQUIRE COST SHARING? __________________________________

## DETERMINE IF THE REQUEST FOR PROPOSAL IS RIGHT FOR YOU

It is imperative for the applicant to familiarize themselves with eligibility requirements and other criteria related to the organization and grant program from which assistance is sought. Applicants should remember that the basic requirements, application forms, information, deadlines, and procedures vary for each funding agency or organization, even when they are from the same agency. For example, the U.S. Department of Justice Office of Justice Programs has nine offices and bureaus with grant authority, each with its own funding process and forms. Since funding information changes, applicants are strongly encouraged to contact the funding source before preparing an application. Look out for grant information or preparation sessions/seminars/workshops that might be hosted by the funding organization. Once you have completed the evaluation of which grant to move forward with and have your Board of Directors' approval, the next step is to review and analyze the Request for Proposal (RFP).

## WHAT IS A REQUEST FOR PROPOSAL?

The funder initiates the process for the awarding of a grant by publishing a Request for Proposal (RFP), and you respond by submitting a grant proposal to indicate your interest. A Grant Proposal is a funding request. You will be asked for a proposal or an application. Usually, when an organization requests a proposal, they are looking for a more accessible form document where you have more control over what you include in the request. An application is similar but the funder will have forms for you to complete. Documents included in an application are strictly limited. Grant funders typically receive numerous grant applications, and the review process can be time-consuming.

When preparing a proposal in response to an RFP, it is important to carefully review all of the guidelines and instructions provided by the funder. This includes understanding the funder's priorities, guidelines for proposal content and format, budget requirements, and any additional requirements or restrictions. It is also important to pay attention to the smallest details, such as font size, margins, and page limits. Even a small mistake or deviation from the instructions could result in your proposal being rejected without consideration. To ensure a successful proposal, it may be helpful to work with a team or consultant with experience in responding to RFPs. They can provide additional insights and guidance on the specific requirements of the funder and help you craft a competitive proposal that meets their needs and objectives.

## Example of an RFP from a Foundation

# Kendal Charitable Funds Promising Innovations
# 2022 Grant-Seeker Guidelines

April 2022

**Please read the guidelines thoroughly before proceeding to the registration and online Letter of Intent forms, available via link at the end of these guidelines.**

**Kendal Charitable Funds, via the Lloyd Lewis Fund for Promising Innovations,** is seeking ideas that can enhance the lives of an aging population through services and research. We are interested in developing new understandings and awareness of issues and opportunities in support of this initiative. We will give priority to projects that have significant potential for change and replication. To learn more about Kendal Charitable Funds and the Lloyd Lewis Fund for Promising Innovations, including prior funded projects, visit our website: https://www.kendal.org/kendal-charitable-funds/impacting-lives/.

**The 2022 grant program will focus on the following topic:**

National workforce shortages are straining the U. S. healthcare system. The shortage of skilled workers is particularly pronounced in the fields of elderly care and is compounded by the COVID-19 pandemic. In addition, many Americans are unaware of the wide range of professional opportunities and careers available in the field of aging services. Some hold negative views about the field.

"Overall, long-term care workforce levels are at their lowest in 15 years, with 409,100 jobs lost between February 2020 and January 2022. The decline has been especially noticeable in skilled nursing, which experienced a 15% workforce decline during that time, according to BLS data. Home health saw a 1.7% decline." https://www.mcknightsseniorliving.com/home/news/long-term-care-workforce-challenges-remain-at-crisis-level/

"A lack of interested or qualified candidates and unemployment benefits discouraging people were cited as the two biggest obstacles for hiring new staff."
https://www.mcknights.com/news/just-1-of-nursing-homes-are-fully-staffed/

The need to recruit and retain talented and committed individuals into the field of aging services is great and immediate.

**We seek proposals that address two or more of the identified immediate needs, through creative, innovative, and replicable strategies and/or programs in the senior living industry and/or related services field that:**

1. **Retain members of the current workforce through positive work experiences**
2. **Recruits and nurtures new members of the senior living workforce**
3. **Builds future employment opportunities and career pathways**
4. **Promotes positive images of employment opportunities and careers in senior living**

**Definitions:**

- **"Senior living industry and/or related services": residential living communities, professional at-home care service providers; adult day programs.**

---

## Eligibility

**The following types of organizations are eligible to apply:**

- 501(c)(3) nonprofits
- 7871 federally recognized Tribal government status

**The following applications will NOT be considered:**

- No grants will be made to institutions which, in policy or practice, discriminate on the basis of race, creed, gender, or sexual orientation.
- In order to concentrate funds on the types of programs identified, it is necessary to specify the kinds of projects we do not fund. These include but are not limited to: support of sectarian religious activities, individual grants, endowment or debt reduction, loans, fellowships, out-of-area-travel, proprietary enterprises, political lobbying or any other political activities.
- Capital requests (defined as support for endowment, construction or equipment) are outside the guidelines of the Lloyd Lewis Fund for Promising Innovations and will not be considered.
- Projects must not be connected in any way with a Kendal Affiliate.

---

## EXERCISE 1.1: WHAT IS AN RFP?

Sometimes you can give your proposal a slight advantage if you can prove to your funders that you speak their language. Read your RFP carefully. What jargon do they use to describe their award in the RFP? Do they use any buzzwords? What Technical Lingo appears throughout the RFP? It might also be very helpful to study the organization to see what terminology in their policy or mission statements are repeated in the RFP. List any critical terms below that you could include in your proposal sections.

After identifying the critical words in your RFP, the next step is to carefully review the instructions, dollar limitations, and contact information for questions. It can be helpful to categorize and color code the RFP for easy reference. Once you have a solid understanding of the RFP requirements, the next step is to assess your grant proposal. Before writing your proposal, you need to answer key questions and gather the necessary data to support your proposal. This will ensure that your proposal is well-researched and tailored to the specific needs of the funder. Attention to detail and thoroughness are critical to the success of your grant proposal

## EXERCISE 1.2: ASSESSING YOUR GRANT PROPOSAL

Why is your project needed? What societal problem(s) does it solve?

How do you intend to solve these problems?

What short-term goals are you trying to reach? How will you achieve them?

What long-term goals are you trying to reach? How will you achieve them?

What is your project design? What will the project accomplish? How will you achieve these goals? Who will do the work? What is the timeline?

What is your organization's capacity to do the work? How does this project fit with your organization's mission and experience?

How will you evaluate the project's success?

What kind of budget will you need to do the work effectively?

In the planning stage, it's essential to develop a logic model as the last step. A logic model helps to outline the steps of your project, making it easier to write a clear and concise proposal. It's a visual and systematic way to present the relationships between the resources needed to operate the program, the planned activities, and the desired outcomes or changes. This model provides a shared understanding of your project's overall structure and can be useful for communicating your plan to stakeholders and funders.

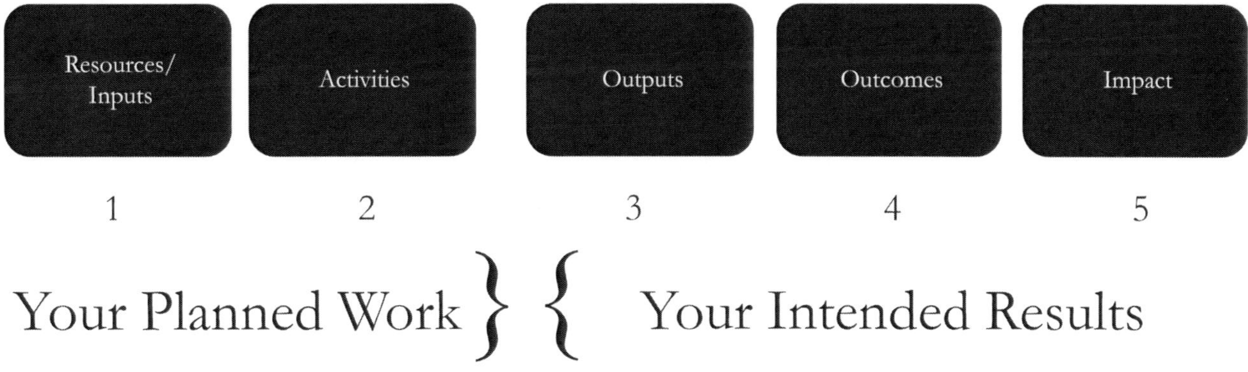


A logic model is a basic yet essential tool in program planning, as it provides a clear and concise understanding of the sequence of activities that are expected to bring about change and the results the program aims to achieve. It can be represented in a visual format using words and/or images to illustrate the relationships among the resources, activities, and outcomes of the program.

The Basic Logic Model components shown in Figure 2 above are described below. These components illustrate the connection between your planned work and your intended results. They are depicted numerically by steps one through five. **YOUR PLANNED WORK** describes what resources you think you need to implement your program and what you intend to do.

1. **Resources** include the human, financial, organizational, and community resources a program has available to direct toward doing the work. Sometimes this component is referred to as Input.
2. **Program Activities** are what the program does with the resources. **Activities** are the processes, tools, events, technology, and actions that are an intentional part of the program implementation. These interventions are used to bring about the intended program changes or results.

**YOUR INTENDED RESULTS** include the program's desired results (outputs, outcomes, and impact). This should align with the funder's desired result should there be any.

3. **Outputs** are the direct products of program activities and may include types, levels, and targets of services to be delivered by the program.
4. **Outcomes** are the specific changes in program participants' behavior, knowledge, skills, status, and level of functioning. Outcomes can also be deliverables or physical products rendered or produced. Short-term outcomes should be attainable within one to three years, while longer-term outcomes should be achievable within four to six years. The logical progression from short-term to long-term outcomes should be reflected in the impact.
5. **Impact** is the fundamental intended or unintended change occurring in organizations, communities, or systems due to program activities within seven to 10 years.

The term logic model is frequently used interchangeably with the term program theory in the evaluation field. Logic models can be referred to as theory because they describe how a program works and to what end.

The purpose of a logic model is to provide stakeholders with a road map describing the sequence of related events connecting the need for the planned program with the program's desired results. Mapping a proposed program helps visualize and understand how human and financial investments can contribute to achieving your intended program goals and can lead to program improvements. A logic model brings program concepts and dreams to life. It lets stakeholders try the idea for size and apply theories to a model or picture of how the program would function. The following example shows how the logic model approach works.

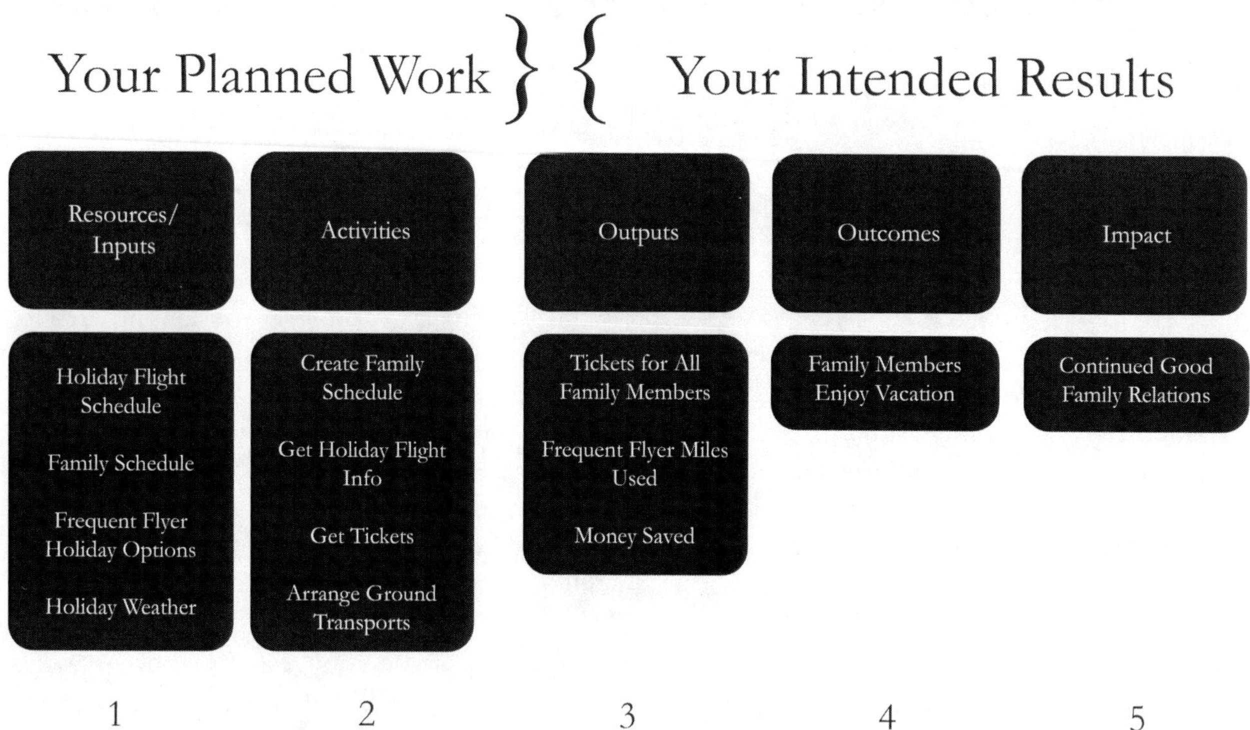


In this example, the results of our activities – or outputs – are mostly information, such as family schedules, flight schedules, and cost information based on the trip's time frame. This information helps identify outcomes or immediate goals. For instance, if we make reservations as soon as possible, we can find flights with available frequent flier slots and probably have more options for flights that fit within the time frame. Knowing this, our outcomes improve – reservations made well in advance result in flight schedules and airline costs that suit our timeline and travel budget. The longer-term impact of our trip is not an issue here but might be projected as continued good family relationships the following year.

Applying a simple logic model to-plan a trip produced tangible benefits. The logic model highlights how gathering information to influence our decisions about resources allowed us to meet our stated goals. Applying this process consistently throughout our trip planning, positions us for success by laying out the best course of action and giving us benchmarks for measuring progress. When we touch down in Charlotte and change planes for Cincinnati, we know we're on the path to Des Moines.

The next couple of exercises will help you prepare your logic model.

## EXERCISE 1.3: LOGIC MODEL DEVELOPMENT EXERCISE

Use the following chart to start making notes for your logic model.

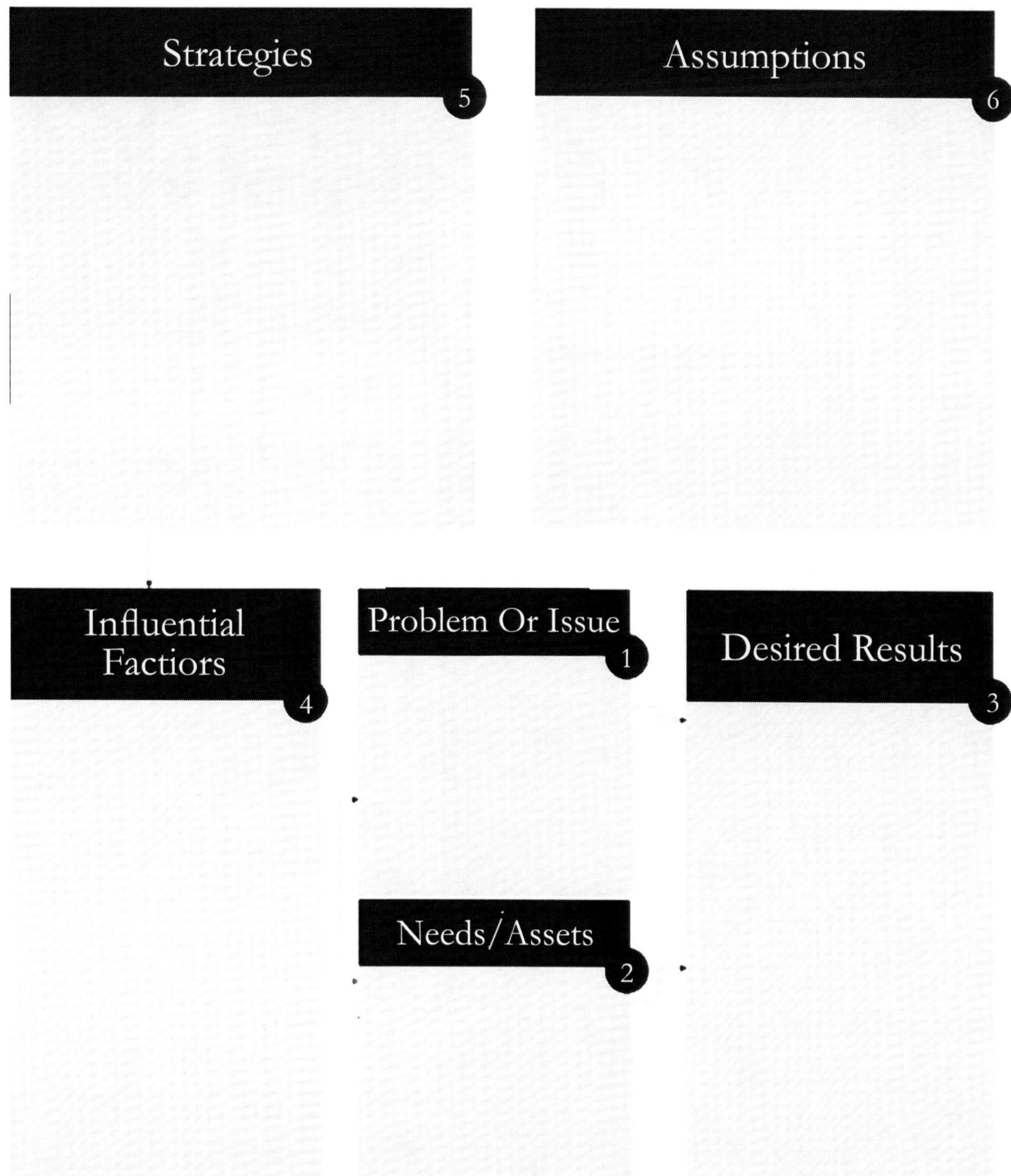

## EXERCISE 1.4: LOGIC MODEL EXERCISE

Using your notes from the previous exercise, complete your logic model using the template below:

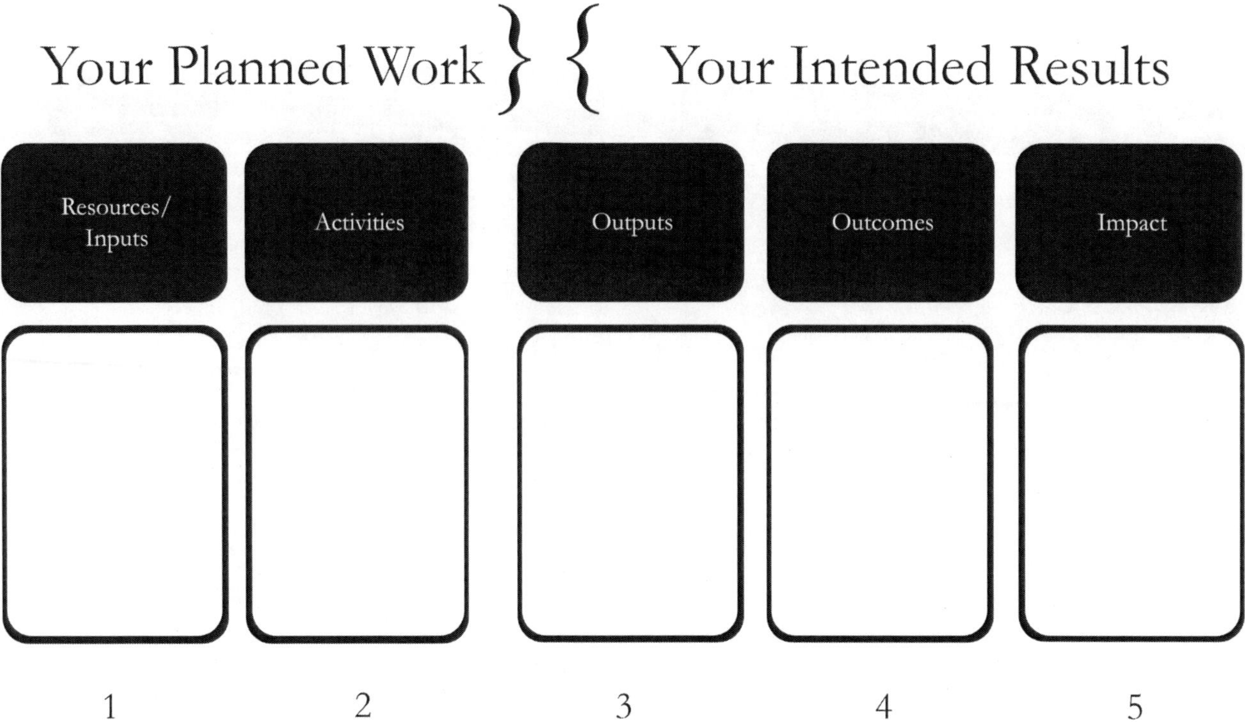


Once you have developed your logic model, it is important to evaluate it to ensure that it is effective and aligned with your program goals. Evaluation of the logic model involves assessing whether it accurately represents the program and its components, and whether it effectively communicates how the program will achieve its intended outcomes. It is also important to evaluate whether the logic model is feasible, given the available resources, and whether it adequately addresses potential challenges and barriers that may arise during program implementation.

Evaluation of the logic model is an ongoing process that involves continuous monitoring and adjustment to ensure that it remains relevant and effective. As the program evolves and new information becomes available, it may be necessary to revise and update the logic model to reflect these changes. By regularly evaluating and adjusting the logic model, program managers can ensure that their programs remain focused, efficient, and effective in achieving their desired outcomes.

## EXERCISE 1.5: LOGIC MODEL EVALUATION

Use the following checklist to evaluate your logic model.

| Criteria | Yes | Not Yet | Comments/Revisions |
|---|---|---|---|
| 1. A variety of audiences are considered when specifying credible outputs, outcomes, and inputs. | ☐ | ☐ | |
| 2. Target participants and/ or partners are described and quantified as outputs (e.g., 100 teachers from 5 rural high schools). | ☐ | ☐ | |
| 3. The duration of the intervention or treatment is appropriate for the type of participant targeted (e.g. | ☐ | ☐ | |
| 4. Outcomes reflect reasonable, progressive steps that participants can make toward longer-term results. | ☐ | ☐ | |
| 5. Outcomes address participants' awareness, attitudes, perceptions, knowledge, skills, and/ or behavior. | ☐ | ☐ | |
| 6. Outcomes are within the scope of the program's control or sphere of reasonable influence. | ☐ | ☐ | |
| 7. It seems fair or reasonable to hold the program accountable for specified outcomes. | ☐ | ☐ | |
| 8. The outcomes are specific, measurable, action-oriented, realistic, and timely. | ☐ | ☐ | |
| 9. The outcomes are achievable within the funding and reporting periods specified. | ☐ | ☐ | |

| | | | |
|---|---|---|---|
| 10. The impact, as specified, is not beyond the program's scope to achieve. | ☐ | ☐ | |
| 11. Major activities needed to implement the program are listed. | ☐ | ☐ | |
| 12. Resources match the type of program. | ☐ | ☐ | |
| 13. All activities have sufficient and appropriate resources. | ☐ | ☐ | |
| 14. The problems to be solved/or issues to be addressed by the planned program are clearly stated. | ☐ | ☐ | |
| 15. There is a specific, transparent connection between the identified community needs/assets and the problems to be solved (or issues to be addressed). | ☐ | ☐ | |
| 16. Indicators are SMART–Specific, Measurable, Action-oriented, Realistic, and Timed. | ☐ | ☐ | |
| 17. The cost of collecting data on the indicators is within the evaluation budget. | ☐ | ☐ | |
| 18. It is clear what data collection, management, and analysis strategies will be most appropriate for each indicator. | ☐ | ☐ | |

## SUMMARY

While it may seem like the planning phase has a lot of steps and details that need to be considered.... it does! Yet, without taking the initial steps upfront, you will waste a lot of your nonprofit's time and resources. Over the years, I have worked with nonprofits that were not grant-ready. The biggest mistake they made was not collecting data or the correct data. They were initially so focused on start-up and receiving their 501c(3) that they did not think about setting future goals. This is understandable because many nonprofits are cash-strapped, volunteer-based, or solely board-run. While one might say if a nonprofit is cash-strapped, why wouldn't they want to apply for a grant? When funders analyze a grant application, they often ask for the nonprofit's most recent financial statements. While funders will not expect nonprofits to be flush with cash, they will look to see if the nonprofit is reasonably solid. For a nonprofit, receiving a grant from a funder is like receiving start-up investment funds for a for-profit. The only difference is that the funder is not expecting a return on the dollars they invest but expecting the program or service to sustain itself upon completion of the grant. Therefore, as soon as one can, strategic planning is needed for financial diversification

# CHAPTER TWO
# Letter of Inquiry / Pre-Application

Most RFPs require a letter of inquiry or intent (the term is used interchangeably) describing your interest in the grant proposal. Within this letter, you will discuss how your organization aligns with the needs of the RFP. These letters are often the first contact an applicant will have with a funder. Some grant funders will require you to submit this letter before completing the grant application. In some cases, you will not be allowed to submit a complete grant application until the funder approves your letter of inquiry. Alternatively, many foundations are now using pre-applications instead of a letter of intent. The pre-application is a shorter version of the complete application.

July 13, 2020

Mario Acosta-Velez
Community Relations Manager
Verizon Foundation

Dear Mr. Acosta-Velez,

My name is Anica Zlotescu, I am employed at Learning Is For Tomorrow (LIFT) as a Blind/Deaf Instructional Coordinator. LIFT is a 501(c)(3) community-based nonprofit adult literacy organization located in Baltimore City, Maryland. I am writing to inquire if the Verizon Foundation would consider a grant proposal for technological upgrades to current network infrastructure so that LIFT can continue to serve adult learners in Baltimore via remote instruction.

LIFT has been providing literacy services to Baltimore City residents since 1988 and is the city's oldest operating literacy organization. LIFT provides adult literacy instruction, computer/ technology training and life-skills instruction to adults who have not received a high school diploma or who have limited literacy abilities. According to the 2014-2018 American Community Survey 5-Year Estimates (ACS 2014-2018), in Baltimore City, 64,129 adults age 25 and older (approximately 15.1% of the 25 and older adult population) lack a high school diploma. LIFT has traditionally served over 300 adult learners per year who are at the lowest income levels and at the lowest literacy ability levels.

The majority of LIFT students face many barriers to learning. These challenges include suspected/diagnosed learning disabilities, physical challenges, learners who are Deaf/Hard of Hearing and those who are Blind/Low-Vision. In Baltimore, 56,482 adults ages 18-64 have some sort of disability (ACS 2011-2015). Through a combination of specialized instruction and adaptive technology, LIFT has a proven track record of success in providing adult literacy services in Maryland to adult learners most at-risk.

In FY2021, LIFT anticipates serving approximately 275 learners. Due to the COVID-19 pandemic, it is necessary for us to move from primarily a classroom-based learning model to increased remote online instruction. We want to upgrade to a server-based network which will allow our learners access to educational software and learning materials remotely. In addition, we would like to increase our internet speed to meet higher demands of internet activity.

An upgrade of this capacity will cost LIFT approximately $12,000 for upgrading our network and computer system. If this is an endeavor the Verizon Foundation would consider supporting, we would appreciate the opportunity to submit a grant proposal that would support adult learners in Baltimore City. Thank you for your consideration.

Warmly,
Anica Zlotescu

Applicants should already have their project well-planned, know the total cost, and how much they intend to request from the foundation when preparing a Letter of Intent. The content of a Letter of Intent will introduce the applicant's organization, summarize the project and expected results, and present the total cost of the project and the amount the applicant will request from the foundation if a full proposal is invited. It should be written on the organization's stationery and limited to preferably one, but not more than two pages. The highest-ranking official in the applicant organization should sign it.

The applicant should clearly and directly state that the organization is seeking funding for a project in the first sentence of the Letter of Intent. The applicant might begin the Letter of Inquiry with the statement: I am writing to state our intent to apply for a grant for $300,000 from the ABC Foundation to support meals for homeless men in Cincinnati, Ohio; and conclude the Letter of Intent with the statement: I welcome your invitation to submit a full proposal. The applicant is not making a grant request per se in a Letter of Intent but rather stating the intent to ask. Grantmakers often criticize Letters of Intent, saying applicants do not give enough attention to them. Essentially, the Letter of Intent should provide enough information for the foundation to make a funding decision.

However, at this early stage in the grant-making process, the Letter of Intent serves to screen applicants on a first impression to determine which applicants will be invited to submit full proposals.

## EXERCISE 2.1: LETTER OF INQUIRY

Below are the common elements of the typical letter of inquiry. Should the funding organization require a pre-application instead of a Letter of Intent, many of the same elements will also appear in the pre-application. Under each section, make notes about what you will include in this section.

### Introduction

The introduction is a short executive summary. It includes your organization's name, the amount of money requested, and a description of the project involved. You'll want to indicate how the project aligns with the funder's guidelines and funding interests. The importance of this last part is often overlooked. We want to clearly present the funder with the alignment rather than leaving it up to them to draw conclusions that may or may not be accurate.

______________________________________________

______________________________________________

______________________________________________

______________________________________________

______________________________________________

______________________________________________

### Organizational Description

Be concise and concentrate on your organization's ability to meet your stated needs. Give a brief history of your nonprofit and a capsule of your programs. Make sure to directly connect what you currently do and what you want to accomplish with the requested funding.

______________________________________________

______________________________________________

______________________________________________

______________________________________________

______________________________________________

### Statement of Need

Explain the need that your project can meet. Describe the target population and geographic area. Provide a few significant statistical facts and several examples. You should include research and citations to validate your comments in this section.

______________________________________________

______________________________________________

**Methodology**

How will you solve the need? Describe the project succinctly and include the significant activities, names and titles of key project staff, and your project's objectives.

______________________________________________

______________________________________________

______________________________________________

______________________________________________

______________________________________________

**Summary**

Restate the intent of your project, explain that you are ready to answer additional questions, and thank the funder for their time and consideration. Include attachments that are consistent with the funder's guidelines.

______________________________________________

______________________________________________

______________________________________________

______________________________________________

______________________________________________

A budget may or may not be required for your letter of inquiry. Check the funder's guidelines. Some guidelines are particular, and it is essential to follow them strictly. At a minimum, it is a good idea to think through your numbers on a more detailed level.

**Salaries** ______________________

**Fringe Benefits** ______________________

**Supplies** ______________________

**Minor Equipment** ______________________

**Other Expenses** ______________________

**Indirect Costs** ______________________

**Total Budget** ______________________

It is good practice to review and edit every part of your document as you work through it. It is very helpful to have multiple people check it and also get a laymen's (or outsider's) viewpoint.

## EXERCISE 2.2: LETTER OF INQUIRY EVALUATION

Below is a letter of intent/inquiry evaluation form, which you can use to evaluate your letter before sending it to the funder.

**Letter of Intent / Inquiry Evaluation Form**

| Criteria | Yes | No | Comments/Revisions |
|---|---|---|---|
| Title of the proposed project | | | |
| Background about the non-profit is provided | | | |
| Brief description of the specific project for which funding is sought | | | |
| Identified good alignment between the nonprofit's and the funder's goals | | | |
| The requested funding amount is stated. The amount is reasonable and in alignment with the funder's levels | | | |
| Description of how the objectives and goals of the proposed project relate to those of the funder | | | |
| The nonprofit's mission and strategies are clearly articulated | | | |
| A primary contact for the organization (This person will receive the foundation's reply via email) | | | |

**Additional Comments**

| |
|---|
| |

**Overall Score (1-100) =**

______________________________

## SUMMARY

When writing your Letter of Intent, it is critical to state your ask, the dollar amount needed, and alignment with the f under in your first paragraph. These are not items you want the reviewer to hunt for and can result in your nonprofit not being asked to submit a proposal. From the writers' perspective, you might think staying the dollar amount right up-front may turn the funder away. The writer would want to emotionally connect with the funder before revealing the dollar amount. As long as the amount you are asking for is within the range of the RFP, there is no need to state this upfront. But if you do not express the alignment between the nonprofit and the funder, the funder will draw their own assumptions. Sometimes these assumptions may not be what was intended, so we never want to leave any holes when writing a grant. For these reasons, many funders have turned to pre-applications in place of the Letter of Intent. The pre-application is structured and leaves less room for interpretation.

# CHAPTER THREE
## Proposal Abstract or Summary

The abstract or executive summary is a brief, page-limited overview of what the grant reviewer will find in the complete grant application. Brevity is essential (this section should be no longer than one page unless the guidelines indicate the need for a two-page summary). It's highly recommended that you write (or assemble) your abstract or summary after you've written the entire grant application narrative. (Note: Federal applications often specify a word or line limit for abstracts - typically around 30 lines.)

**Tips for writing the abstract:**

- Write the abstract last.
- Include a sentence from each section.
- Make a good first impression.

**ABSTRACT**

The Efficient Storage Shed Solution (ESSS) is the Black Feather Horse Rescue (BFHR) resolution to resolve the absence of a sufficient storage space to house bulk purchases of grain and feed. As aligned with the priorities of the Brennan Equine Welfare Fund to provide a safe and peaceful environment to equines in rescue shelters, BFHR seeks to construct a durable and clean unit to store grain and feed, which will ultimately improve the quality of grain and feed in order to help ensure the over0all health and well-being of our organization's equine residents.

In addition, the project will address issues of cost and efficiencies as it will allow us to store larger quantities of grain and feed for longer periods of time rather than purchasing grain and feed on a daily basis.

The success of the project will be seen in the health of our equine community and the lowered costs of resources associated with buying bulk grain and feed. These costs will be evaluated on a monthly basis and reported on 6 months after construction of the storage shed.

### EXERCISE 3.1: ABSTRACT OR EXECUTIVE SUMMARY

You can create an abstract or executive summary by pulling the most significant sentences from each critical section in the grant narrative if no specific structure is requested. Take imperative sentences from the following sections, and keep them in the same order in the abstract or executive summary as they appear in the narrative:

**Proposed initiative**: Here, you enter the name of your project or program and the full name of the funding competition you're applying to for grant consideration.

**Introduction of target population**: Copy and paste a sentence or two about who you're planning to target and serve.

**Goals**: Copy and paste your goals from your proposal narrative. These should follow the SMART framework.

**Program measurements and performance targets (also known as objectives)**: Copy and paste your objectives and performance targets from your proposal narrative.

**Plan of action:** Copy and paste the key activities that comprise the program's implementation process.

______________________________________________________________

______________________________________________________________

______________________________________________________________

______________________________________________________________

______________________________________________________________

## SUMMARY

As a grant reviewer, I always start with the budget. If an organization does not have a handle on how much a project and/or program will cost, then there is no use to read the rest. Additionally, operating and grant budgets are often confused, which can indicate a lack of internal financial acumen. However, every grant reviewer is different in what they will prioritize. Every section needs to be given the same amount of focus and energy. Once I complete my review of the budget, I look at the abstract because it provides an overview of the proposal. The abstract will be my roadmap to reviewing the rest of the grant.

# CHAPTER FOUR
# The Problem Statement

Issues that consistently arise in literature, theory, or practice can be formulated into a Problem statement expressing the need for a study. When writing a grant, you must persuade others of the need for the program/service/research. We often do not identify the actual problem but rather what we see on the surface. While this might resolve some short-term issues, the problem will continue to creep back. We therefore need to make sure we are digging deep and uncovering the actual problem.

The difference between a problem statement for generalized research and a small nonprofit lies in the scope and context of the issues being addressed. In generalized research, the problem statement aims to identify and articulate a research gap or a specific problem that needs further investigation. It provides a clear rationale for conducting the study and highlights the significance and relevance of the research problem in the broader context of existing literature, theory, or practice.

On the other hand, for a small nonprofit organization, the problem statement is typically focused on addressing a specific issue or challenge faced by the organization or the community it serves. This problem statement is crucial in grant writing as it seeks to persuade funders or stakeholders of the need for the proposed program or intervention. It should clearly define the problem, its underlying causes, and the potential impact of addressing it.

It is important to note that in both cases, simply addressing the surface-level manifestations of a problem may only provide temporary solutions. To achieve long-term and sustainable outcomes, it is crucial to dig deeper and uncover the root causes of the problem. By understanding the underlying factors contributing to the problem, researchers or nonprofit organizations can develop more effective strategies and interventions that address the core issues and create lasting positive change.

Therefore, whether it is in the context of generalized research or a small nonprofit, it is essential to conduct thorough analysis and investigation to ensure that the identified problem statement accurately reflects the real issues at hand. By doing so, researchers and nonprofit organizations can devise comprehensive and impactful solutions that tackle the root causes and lead to meaningful outcomes.

## EXERCISE 4.1: PROBLEM STATEMENT DEVELOPMENT

The first step to developing your problem statement is asking yourself the following question:

**What is the rationale for doing this project?**

______________________________________________

______________________________________________

______________________________________________

______________________________________________

One must be passionate about the problem, have a strong desire to study and solve the problem, and commit the time and resources to obtain the solution. Answer the following questions before building your problem statement:

**Can the problem be studied?**

- Do you have access to the research population?
- Do you have the time, resources, and skills to conduct the research?

______________________________________________________________________

______________________________________________________________________

______________________________________________________________________

______________________________________________________________________

______________________________________________________________________

**Should you study the problem?**

- Does it advance knowledge?
- Does it contribute to practice?

______________________________________________________________________

______________________________________________________________________

______________________________________________________________________

______________________________________________________________________

______________________________________________________________________

The problem explains the rationale for the study, validates its importance, and determines the research design or program setup.

## The Problem Statement

The problem statement is a crucial component of grant writing as it serves several important purposes. It not only explains the rationale for conducting the study but also validates the significance of the research, determines the research design, and ensures the reliability of the findings. A well-crafted problem statement enables the reader to understand the purpose of the study and its relevance within the larger context. It should address a significant problem in a unique and innovative manner, contributing to both knowledge and practice.

Before writing the problem statement, grant writers need to carefully assess the situation, explore potential problems, and devise a strategic plan. Taking the time to do this initial groundwork is beneficial, as it eases the process of completing the rest of the grant proposal. However, creating effective problem statements can be challenging and time-consuming. Given that the problem statement drives the entire study, including the choice of research design and the resulting conclusions, it is vital to invest effort in writing a clear and comprehensive problem statement. Without a well-defined problem statement, research results can be deemed invalid, biased, or inconclusive.

To ensure success, grant writers should revise their problem statements multiple times until they achieve a paragraph that includes all the critical elements. This iterative process helps refine the problem statement, making it more impactful and aligned with the objectives of the study. By emphasizing the importance of a well-crafted problem statement, grant writers can increase the likelihood of securing funding and conducting research that addresses significant issues in a meaningful way.

### Building the Problem Statement

In 250 words or less (one or two paragraphs), the problem statement should convince the audience that this study MUST be done and CAN be solved. The problem statement is supported by scholarly evidence that this problem is serious and needs further investigation. The problem statement should have four parts:

- A statement of the general problem.
- A statement of the specific problem.
- An introductory statement describing the research design.
- A statement identifying the population to be studied.

If the problem is sound, the researcher should be able to explain it to a stranger in an elevator between the second and third floors. If the problem can be stated in one sentence, and the stranger understands the situation, the researcher has an excellent first line of the problem statement.

The second line of a problem statement states what needs to be accomplished to solve the problem and should communicate the research design. Selecting the right research design is critical. If the research design does not match the problem, it will be difficult, if not impossible, to conduct the research study. This is a great time to consider consulting a statistician. The second line should specify the researcher's approach to exploring the problem.

## EXERCISE 4.2: PROBLEM STATEMENT EXERCISE

Let's practice! Read the following scenario and then write a short problem statement (no more than five sentences) that addresses the following three questions:

- What is the problem you're trying to solve?
- Why should we care about this problem?
- How will you solve this problem?

### Practice Scenario

You want to teach work readiness to disabled high school students and assist in their school-to-work transition. Your school has initiated innovative career awareness programs in the past. Students with disabilities make up 10% of the school's population. Many learning disabilities go undiagnosed but limit students' performance at school and work. People with disabilities are often under-employed and have higher unemployment and poverty rates than people without disabilities. Your town has small employers who worry about how the ADA will affect them. The unemployment rate in your town is 4.5%. Good-paying jobs are often not available to teenagers because employers prefer to hire people they think will be more mature.

## *SUMMARIZING A FEW BEST PRACTICES FOR PROBLEM STATEMENTS*

- Problem statement is 200 – 250 words in length or an average of 1/2 to 3/4 of a page (double-spaced).
- Problem statement includes four parts:
  - o General problem/observation identifying the need for the study
  - o Specific problem proposed for research
  - o Introductory words describing the research method and design
  - o Includes general population of the proposed study
- Problem statement is clear and concise and reflects scholarly writing
- Includes appropriate references to support all assertions
- References are no more than five years old, if at all possible
- Problem statement is written in 3rd person
- Problem statement ends with a strong statement about why business leaders should care about your research - what information/data it may provide and how this will help them.

## EXERCISE 4.3: PROBLEM STATEMENT CHECKLIST

Answer the following questions to help guide you in writing your problem statement.

**What is the problem?**

Describe the situation that needs improvement. What is happening that should not be happening, or what is not happening, that should be happening? What is the evidence of the problem? When composing the problem statement, researchers should show the problem. That is, researchers need to avoid simply explaining the problem and, instead, should describe the problem by detailing its effects and evidence.

**What ill effects does this problem create within a society and/or its subsets?**

Determining these effects will aid in researching and composing the background section.

**Where (professions, sub-specialties, etc.) is the problem found? Who would request a study of the problem?**

Determining the problem's influence will aid in researching and composing the literature review.

**What journal(s) would be interested in publishing this study?**

Finding an opportunity for publication will aid in researching and composing the literature review.

**What topics, subjects, or issues (stock market, drugs, violence, language development, assessment, euthanasia, etc.) are involved?**

Defining all related issues will aid in researching the literature review.

**What has already been done about the problem? What has not been done?**

Examining the problem's history will aid in researching the literature review.

**What harm could be done if this study was NOT conducted?**

Determining potential outcomes will help define the purpose and significance.

**Why are you interested in this problem? Why would someone else be interested in this problem?**

Determining interest will aid in describing the study's significance.

**Who is affected? What group would care about this problem?**

Determining the affected parties will help define the sample, population, and significance.

**What part of the problem can this study help solve?**

Will it assist others in making wiser choices? Will it help debunk a myth? Understanding how a study can potentially address a problem will help define the study's purpose and significance.

**What value will the research create?**

Will it clarify an ambiguous point or theory, look at a new aspect of a problem, or aid in a necessary decision-making process? Determining the potential value of a study will help define its purpose and significance.

**What needs to be done to investigate the problem?**

Which verb best describes the focus of the study's research: analyze, describe, evaluate, test, understand, determine, define, establish, etc.? Understanding the investigative approach is crucial for determining the methodology and instruments to be used in the study.

**How does the study relate to the development or refinement of theory?**

Understanding the potential contribution will aid in designing the theoretical framework.

**What could result from this study?**

Which verb best describes the study's trajectory: clarify, debunk, relieve, assist, create, recommend, etc.? Understanding potential outcomes will help with the interpretation of results.

## EXERCISE 4.4: PROBLEM STATEMENT EVALUATION

Once you have written your problem statement, this is a good time to do another review and edit session. Having someone with an unbiased view review would also be beneficial at this point. The following will help to evaluate your problem statement:

**Problem:**

______________________________

______________________________

______________________________

______________________________

______________________________

**Score:** 1 2 3 4 5

**Need:**

______________________________

______________________________

______________________________

______________________________

______________________________

**Score:** 1 2 3 4 5

**Objective:**

______________________________

______________________________

______________________________

______________________________

______________________________

Score: 1 2 3 4 5

**Method**:

________________________________________

________________________________________

________________________________________

________________________________________

________________________________________

Score: 1 2 3 4 5

**Evaluation:**

________________________________________

________________________________________

________________________________________

________________________________________

________________________________________

Score: 1 2 3 4 5

The problem statement is the most critical element of grant writing. The problem statement explains the rationale for the study, validates its importance, determines the research design, and ensures reliability. *Problems, problems, problems all day long… Will my problems work out right or wrong?* A strong and passionate problem statement will deliver the study's passion and set the stage for the solution (right or wrong).

## SUMMARY

The problem statement is a critical component of the grant. Learning to define the problem statement is challenging because, often, what we believe the problem is not always accurate. This is because we are only looking at the problem from our perspective. So before writing this, research is needed to narrow down the problem and gain information from different perspectives. Once we have this narrowed down, we can gain clarity. It is essential not to be looking at your problem from 29,000 feet in the sky but rather scrutinize it at a microscopic level.

When writing my dissertation for my doctorate, I thought I had the perfect problem statement. I wanted to research Women in Leadership. My mentor said wonderful, what are you going to study because that is too broad. After researching peer-reviewed journals and speaking with people from different industries and levels, I finally clarified how to narrow it down. My final problem statement read:

*The specific problem is that gender barriers prevent qualified and experienced women from achieving corporate officer positions.*

So you can see how this evolved and was narrowed down. It was like looking down a funnel and seeing clarity at the end. When writing your grant, you want to ensure this level of clarity.

# CHAPTER FIVE
# Goals and Action Plans

When defining your goals, they should be based on SMART objectives. Goals are general, whereas objectives are more specific. SMART objectives are Specific, Measurable, Attainable, Realistic, and Timely. Let us consider each characteristic in more detail.

**Specific**: A specific goal is much more likely to be accomplished than a general one. To set a specific goal, you must answer the six W questions:

- WHO: Who is involved?
- WHAT: What do I want to accomplish?
- WHERE: Identify a location.
- WHEN: Establish a time frame.
- WHICH: Identify requirements and constraints.
- WHY: Specific reasons, purpose, or benefits of accomplishing the goal.

**Measurable** - Establish concrete criteria for measuring progress toward each objective you set. When you measure your progress, you stay on track, reach your target dates, and experience the exhilaration of achievement that spurs you on to the continued effort required to reach your goal. To determine if your objective is measurable, ask questions such as:

- How much?
- How many?
- How will I know when it is accomplished?

**Attainable** – When you identify the most important objectives, you begin to figure out ways to realize them. Focusing on clearly defined goals and objectives allows you to develop the attitudes, abilities, skills, and financial capacity to reach them. You start seeing previously overlooked opportunities to bring yourself closer to achieving your goals as they are now better defined. You can attain almost any goal you set when you plan your steps wisely and establish a time frame that allows you to carry out those steps. Goals that may have seemed far away and out of reach eventually move closer and become attainable when you break them down into small attainable steps. With each conquered step you gain momentum and you might feel your goals shrink because you grow and expand in experience to match them.

**Realistic** - To be realistic, a goal must represent an objective toward which you are both willing and able to work. A goal can be both high and realistic; you are the only one who can decide just how high your goal should be. A low goal exerts a low motivational force so lofty goals are frequently easier to reach due to exerting a high motivational force. But be sure that every achieved goal represents substantial progress

**Timely** – A goal should be grounded within a time frame. There's no sense of urgency with no time frame tied to a specific goal or objective.

**T** can also stand for **Tangible** – A goal is tangible when you can experience it with one of the senses: taste, touch, smell, sight, or hearing. When your goal is tangible, you have a better chance of making it specific, measurable, and thus attainable.

### Example of a Short-term SMART Goal

Short-term goals should be attainable within six months to a year.

#### Short-Term Goal #1:

**What is your primary short-term goal?** To create two additional workstations using general operating funds in the existing office space at 710 4th Avenue, Venice, CA, by May 2nd for two new employees.

1. **Is it specific?** (Who? What? Where? When? Why?) Yes, two new employees require a workstation with a computer and telephone extension within the main office space.
2. **Is it measurable? How will I measure progress?** (How many? How much?) Yes, this is measurable: as a workstation has a physical form, it will be evident that the goal has been reached when each new employee works at their station.
3. **Is it attainable?** (Can this really happen? Attainable with enough effort? What steps are involved?) Yes, there are carved-out spaces to create these workstations, and existing donor/development funds will cover operational expenses.
4. **Is it realistic?** (What knowledge, skills, and abilities are necessary to reach this goal?) Yes, this is a realistic goal. We have funds to cover the cost of the equipment. We have a contracted technician who will perform installation/set-up services.
5. **Is it time bound?** (Can I set fixed deadlines? What are the deadlines?) Yes, the two new workstations will be ready by May 2, 2015.

### Example of a Long-term SMART Goal

Long-term goals should be attainable within two to five years.

**What is your primary long-term goal?** Within three to five years, we can sustainably offer the Parent Advocacy Program to 100 low-income families and children enrolled at the Elizabeth Peabody House, Somerville, MA. The program's success will be evidenced through participant accounts and surveys. It will be funded through donations and other funding streams. In alignment with the demands and needs of the program, one volunteer coordinator and five social workers will be engaged to develop community workshops in collaboration with local early educators. The program will also be extended to families in the Greater Boston Area.

1. **Is it specific?** (Who? What? When? Where? Why?) Yes. The participants will be Low-income families; the staff will be based at the Elizabeth Peabody House. The location will remain in Somerville, MA. The purpose is to support impoverished children in the community and give them the essential items and their parents the knowledge that will propel them to thrive.
2. **Is it measurable? How will I measure progress?** (How many? How Much?) Yes, both elements

of the programs can be measured through an account of participants and service surveys.

3. **Is it attainable?** (Can this really happen? Attainable with enough effort? What steps are involved?) Yes, it is attainable with continued funding, diversity of fundraising strategies, and measures of participant impact.

4. **Is it realistic?** (What knowledge, skills, and abilities are necessary to reach this goal?) Yes, as the program grows, we will need skilled social workers to perform much of the responsibilities required for helping families with the crisis. We will need a volunteer coordinator to help handle the influx of donations and to coordinate meeting times for families to receive items. In conjunction with Early educators, the social worker/ or team of workers will develop appropriate workshops to help educate parents.

5. **Is it time bound?** Yes, the expansion of the program will take three to five years.

## EXERCISE 5.1: DEVELOPING YOUR SMART GOALS

Use this worksheet to identify the specific SMART criteria you will use to write your goal statement.

**Short-Term Goal #1:**

What is your basic short-term goal?

____________________________________________

____________________________________________

1. Is it specific? (Who? What? Where? When? Why?)

____________________________________________

____________________________________________

2. Is it measurable? How will I measure progress? (How many? How much?)

____________________________________________

____________________________________________

3. Is it attainable? (Can this really happen? Attainable with enough effort? What steps are involved?)

____________________________________________

____________________________________________

4. Is it realistic? (What knowledge, skills, and abilities are necessary to reach this goal?)

____________________________________________

____________________________________________

5. Is it time bound? (Can I set fixed deadlines? What are the deadlines?)

____________________________________________

**SHORT-TERM GOAL #2:**

What is your basic short-term goal?

______________________________________________

______________________________________________

1. Is it specific? (Who? What? Where? When? Why?)

______________________________________________

______________________________________________

2. Is it measurable? How will I measure progress? (How many? How much?)

______________________________________________

______________________________________________

3. Is it attainable? (Can this really happen? Attainable with enough effort? What steps are involved?)

______________________________________________

______________________________________________

4. Is it realistic? (What knowledge, skills, and abilities are necessary to reach this goal?)

______________________________________________

______________________________________________

5. Is it time bound? (Can I set fixed deadlines? What are the deadlines?)

______________________________________________

______________________________________________

**SHORT-TERM GOAL #3:**

What is your basic short-term goal?

______________________________________________

______________________________________________

1. Is it specific? (Who? What? Where? When? Why?)

2. Is it measurable? How will I measure progress? (How many? How much?)

3. Is it attainable? (Can this really happen? Attainable with enough effort? What steps are involved?)

4. Is it realistic? (What knowledge, skills, and abilities are necessary to reach this goal?)

5. Is it time bound? (Can I set fixed deadlines? What are the deadlines?)

**Long-Term Goal #1:**

What is your basic long-term goal?

1. Is it specific? (Who? What? Where? When? Why?)

2. Is it measurable? How will I measure progress? (How many? How much?)

3. Is it attainable? (Can this really happen? Attainable with enough effort? What steps are involved?)

4. Is it realistic? (What knowledge, skills, and abilities are necessary to reach this goal?)

5. Is it time bound? (Can I set fixed deadlines? What are the deadlines?)

**Long-Term Goal #2:**

What is your basic long-term goal?

1. Is it specific? (Who? What? Where? When? Why?)

2. Is it measurable? How will I measure progress? (How many? How much?)

3. Is it attainable? (Can this really happen? Attainable with enough effort? What steps are involved?)

4. Is it realistic? (What knowledge, skills, and abilities are necessary to reach this goal?)

5. Is it time bound? (Can I set fixed deadlines? What are the deadlines?)

**Long-Term Goal #3:**

What is your basic long-term goal?

______________________________________________

______________________________________________

1. Is it specific? (Who? What? Where? When? Why?)

______________________________________________

______________________________________________

2. Is it measurable? How will I measure progress? (How many? How much?)

______________________________________________

______________________________________________

3. Is it attainable? (Can this really happen? Attainable with enough effort? What steps are involved?)

______________________________________________

______________________________________________

4. Is it realistic? (What knowledge, skills, and abilities are necessary to reach this goal?)

______________________________________________

______________________________________________

5. Is it time bound? (Can I set fixed deadlines? What are the deadlines?)

______________________________________________

______________________________________________

Now that you have made some notes about your short and long-term goals, it is time to take it to the next level. We need to formalize the plans and define the necessary action steps. A goal without action steps is nothing more than a notion or dream. Action steps break the goal down into achievable segments, measure your progress, and keep the momentum going. They give you concrete plans for reaching your goal and in doing so help you stay focused. Action steps are what turn dreams into realities. And action steps with dates attached to them, help you stay on task and assure small victories along the way to your ultimate goal -which (I hope it goes without saying) also needs a target date associated with it!

## EXERCISE 5.2: FINALIZING YOUR GOALS AND ADDING ACTION STEPS

Use this worksheet to finalize your SMART goals and outline the specific steps you need to take to achieve your goals.

SHORT-TERM GOAL #1:

______________________________________________

______________________________________________

______________________________________________

| Action Steps | Deadline | Necessary Resources | Potential Challanges | Potential Support | Result |
|---|---|---|---|---|---|
| What needs to be done? | When should this step be completed? | What resources can you use to complete this step? | Are there any potential challanges that may impede completion? How Will you overco-me them? | What people in your life can support you to complete this action step? What can they do to support you? | Was this step successfully completed? Were any new steps identified in the process? |
| • | • | • | • | • | • |
| • | • | • | • | • | • |
| • | • | • | • | • | • |
| • | • | • | • | • | • |
| • | • | • | • | • | • |
| • | • | • | • | • | • |

Short-Term Goal #2:

| Action Steps | Deadline | Necessary Resources | Potential Challanges | Potential Support | Result |
|---|---|---|---|---|---|
| What needs to be done? | When should this step be completed? | What resources can you use to complete this step? | Are there any potential challanges that may impede completion? How Will you overco-me them? | What people in your life can support you to complete this action step? What can they do to support you? | Was this step successfully completed? Were any new steps identified in the process? |

SHORT-TERM GOAL #3:

| Action Steps | Deadline | Necessary Resources | Potential Challanges | Potential Support | Result |
|---|---|---|---|---|---|
| What needs to be done? | When should this step be completed? | What resources can you use to complete this step? | Are there any potential challanges that may impede completion? How Will you overco-me them? | What people in your life can support you to complete this action step? What can they do to support you? | Was this step successfully completed? Were any new steps identified in the process? |

Long-Term Goal #1:

| Action Steps | Deadline | Necessary Resources | Potential Challanges | Potential Support | Result |
|---|---|---|---|---|---|
| What needs to be done? | When should this step be completed? | What resources can you use to complete this step? | Are there any potential challanges that may impede completion? How Will you overco-me them? | What people in your life can support you to complete this action step? What can they do to support you? | Was this step successfully completed? Were any new steps identified in the process? |

LONG-TERM GOAL #2:

| Action Steps | Deadline | Necessary Resources | Potential Challanges | Potential Support | Result |
|---|---|---|---|---|---|
| What needs to be done? | When should this step be completed? | What resources can you use to complete this step? | Are there any potential challanges that may impede completion? How Will you overco-me them? | What people in your life can support you to complete this action step? What can they do to support you? | Was this step successfully completed? Were any new steps identified in the process? |

LONG-TERM GOAL #3:

| Action Steps | Deadline | Necessary Resources | Potential Challanges | Potential Support | Result |
| --- | --- | --- | --- | --- | --- |
| What needs to be done? | When should this step be completed? | What resources can you use to complete this step? | Are there any potential challanges that may impede completion? How Will you overco-me them? | What people in your life can support you to complete this action step? What can they do to support you? | Was this step successfully completed? Were any new steps identified in the process? |

## SUMMARY

SMART objectives are an effective framework for defining goals that are specific, measurable, attainable, realistic, and timely. When setting goals, it is important to ensure they are specific, answering questions such as who is involved, what needs to be accomplished, where it will take place, when it should be achieved, which requirements and constraints exist, and why it is important. Measurable goals establish concrete criteria for tracking progress, while attainable goals are within reach and can be broken down into smaller steps. Realistic goals represent objectives that are both high and feasible, requiring the necessary effort and resources to achieve them. Timely goals are grounded within a defined time frame, and tangible goals can be experienced through the senses. The effectiveness of a problem statement and the success of a grant depend on the clarity and comprehensiveness of the stated goals. Taking the time to craft well-defined problem statements and SMART objectives is crucial for grant writers to secure funding and conduct impactful research.

# CHAPTER SIX
# Statement of Need

If the potential funder reads beyond the executive summary, you have piqued their interest. Your next task is to build on this initial interest in your project by enabling the funder to understand the problem the project will remedy. The need statement will allow the reader to learn more about the issues. It presents the facts and evidence supporting the project's need and establishes that your nonprofit understands the problem and therefore can reasonably address it. You want this section to be concise yet persuasive. Like a good debater, you must assemble all the arguments. Then present them in a logical sequence that will readily convince the reader of their importance.

A Few Best Practices for the Statement of Need

- Do not use jargon
- Spell out acronyms
- Do not assume the reviewer knows about the conditions that prompted the project
- Do not editorialize – State the Facts
- Stick to the main point
- Need should be based on rational terms and not on emotional appeals
- Avoid circular reasoning
- Your solution is not your problem
- Make sure the Statement of Need is locally based and focused
- The need may be a national problem as well but make sure that you establish that it is a local problem through relevant data
- Do not assume that a national problem is automatically a local problem

The need statement should be a direct definition of the problem and is the primary driver of the grant. This is often the starting point for the grant and the first piece a reviewer will look at. Below is an example of a Statement of Need from the Black Feather Horse Rescue:

## STATEMENT OF NEED

The Black Feather Horse Rescue (BFHR) has been striving to provide sanctuary and training for neglected and abused horses throughout the state of Massachusetts since 2004. In 2008 BFHR was able to expand its facility to house and accommodate an increasing number of rescued horses. To properly care for the new arrivals, a larger staff of volunteers and employees was required. By 2009 the required staff and volunteers had been acquired. Thanks to this most recent expansion, Black Feather Horse Rescue has been able to find loving homes for over twenty rescued horses. A dozen still currently reside on the property, some in training as therapeutic companions for the elderly and children with special needs.

The demand for a stable environment in which to house neglected horses has been increasing steadily over the past several years; this becomes especially apparent when coupled with the demand for therapeutic riding and exposure. In order to meet the quality standards required to run a successful equine rescue, BFHR is in constant need of veterinary services, training equipment, lodging stations, and basic feed.

With this in mind, we are requesting the funding for a new pre-built feed shed based on the organization's need for effective storage solutions. BFHR hopes that this new addition will ultimately increase the health of our equines, improve the quality of our grains and feed, and help increase resource and fuel efficiencies to the organization. The storage unit will also add to a more professional atmosphere, allowing visitors to trust and feel the healing properties associated with animal therapy and wilderness exploration. In addition, better care for the horses will help to encourage an increase in adoptions to loving families.

When written well, the Statement of Need should tell the potential funders why they should care about the problem. The Statement of Need should contain data and comparative statistics about the population you are serving. It is helpful to have someone designated to research and collect this data while others continue to work on the grant.

### EXERCISE 6.1: STATEMENT OF NEED DEVELOPMENT EXERCISE

The statement of need should answer the following guiding questions:

**Who is affected by the problem? Describe the "target population" and circumstances.**

____________________________________________________________

____________________________________________________________

____________________________________________________________

____________________________________________________________

**What problem(s) are you going to address?**

**What specific conditions would you like to change?**

**How will making those changes make things better? (Rationale)**

**Where will you get the data? To support this project, what kinds of data can you get/present to support your need/problem?**

When developing your Statement of Need it can be challenging to identify the actual problem. We often only identify aspects we see on the surface, but that is seldom the problem. It is critical to find the true underlying problem; otherwise, you will just be putting a Band-Aid on the problem, and it eventually will reemerge. Let's practice!

## EXERCISE 6.2: STATEMENT OF NEED EXERCISE

Write a statement of need (based on the below scenario) of no more than five sentences that address the following:

- What is the problem you're trying to solve?
- Why should we care about this problem?
- How will you solve this problem?

Draft Statement of Need

______________________________________________________________________

______________________________________________________________________

______________________________________________________________________

______________________________________________________________________

______________________________________________________________________

______________________________________________________________________

______________________________________________________________________

______________________________________________________________________

______________________________________________________________________

______________________________________________________________________

Now let's evaluate this statement of need:

1 = Does not demonstrate Need
2 = Poor job of demonstrating Need
3 = Fair job of demonstrating Need
4 = Good job of demonstrating Need
5 = Excellent job of demonstrating Need

| | | | | | |
|---|---|---|---|---|---|
| How clear and easy it is to read | 1 | 2 | 3 | 4 | 5 |
| How significant the problem is | 1 | 2 | 3 | 4 | 5 |
| How feasible your solution is to carry out | 1 | 2 | 3 | 4 | 5 |
| How much impact your solution will have | 1 | 2 | 3 | 4 | 5 |
| How logically your solution follows from the problem | 1 | 2 | 3 | 4 | 5 |

## SUMMARY

The need statement is a crucial component of a grant proposal that aims to capture the attention and understanding of potential funders. It provides an opportunity to present the problem that the project intends to address, showcasing the nonprofit's comprehension of the issue and its ability to offer a reasonable solution. The need statement should be concise yet persuasive, presenting factual evidence and logical arguments to establish the importance of the problem. Best practices for crafting a compelling need statement include avoiding jargon, explaining acronyms, focusing on facts rather than emotional appeals, staying on topic, avoiding circular reasoning, and ensuring the statement is locally based and supported by relevant data. A well-written need statement should effectively convey why the funders should care about the problem and often serves as the starting point for the grant proposal. It is essential to include data and comparative statistics to provide a clear understanding of the population being served.

# CHAPTER SEVEN
# Evaluation/Outcome and Impact

Outcomes define what you want a program or service to accomplish. As a capacity-building organization, your intended outcomes focus on the impacts or changes that the organization experience due to the influence of your program or service. Another trap many organizations fall into when identifying outcomes is to describe what they have done (i.e., the activities they carried out) rather than the impact of these activities on the client organization. As you become familiar with outcomes, remember that you will not measure many. You'll want to pick a couple most directly connected to your assistance. You can use outcome statements to help you develop your outcomes. Writing an outcome statement can take many forms—the more straightforward, the better.

Outcome or performance indicators must be specific and observable. They answer questions like how you will know when changes have occurred and how you will know when you have achieved the outcomes. Thinking about possible data collection methods will tell you if your indicators are specific enough. Ask questions like these to determine whether your indicators will work:

- How can I see the change? (Through what kind of observation?)
- How can I hear the change? (Through interviews? Focus groups?)
- How can I read the change? (Through surveys? In records?)

The following exercise will help determine what type of data should be collected and how.

## EXERCISE 7.1: EVALUATION/OUTCOMES AND IMPACT

## THE PROCESS

What type of data will be collected?

______________________________

______________________________

______________________________

______________________________

______________________________

Who will collect the data?

How will it be analyzed?

How often will data be collected and analyzed?

## THE IMPACT

What type of data will be collected?

Who will collect the data?

How will it be analyzed?

How often will data be collected and analyzed?

## THE OUTCOME

What type of data will be collected?

Who will collect the data?

____________________

____________________

____________________

____________________

____________________

How will it be analyzed?

____________________

____________________

____________________

____________________

____________________

How often will data be collected and analyzed?

____________________

____________________

____________________

____________________

____________________

How will the analyzed data be used, and by whom? Who will prepare and submit the required reports?

____________________

____________________

____________________

____________________

____________________

Once you have determined the potential outcomes of your grant and what you will evaluate, the next crucial step is to carefully assess your data collection methods. Your data collection process should encompass all the elements outlined in your logic model, including the resources available, activities conducted, outputs delivered, and the degree of accomplishment of your desired outcomes. While your organization's records can provide much of the necessary information for these elements, collecting data for outcomes and indicators requires additional considerations.

To collect indicator data, you have several options at your disposal, such as surveys, interviews, observation, and record or document review. Choosing the most suitable method for data collection requires weighing the advantages and disadvantages associated with each approach. Factors to consider include the type of information needed, as certain outcomes and indicators may lend themselves better to a specific method, while in other cases, multiple methods could be used. Additionally, you should consider the validity and reliability of the methods, as some may generate more accurate and consistent information than others.

- **Type of information needed** — some outcomes and indicators lend themselves to one particular method; in other cases, data could be collected in more than one way
- **Validity and reliability** — some methods generate more accurate and consistent information than others
- **Resources available** —including staff availability and expertise, time, and cost
- **Cultural appropriateness** — using the broadest definition of culture to ensure that the methods fit the language, norms, and values of the individuals and groups from whom you are collecting data

Another critical aspect to take into account is the availability of resources, including staff expertise, time constraints, and associated costs. Selecting a method that aligns with the available resources is crucial to ensure the feasibility of data collection. Furthermore, it is essential to consider cultural appropriateness, which entails ensuring that the chosen methods align with the language, norms, and values of the individuals and groups from whom you are collecting data. By adopting a broad definition of culture, you can ensure that your data collection methods are inclusive and respectful.

In this stage, it is highly recommended to involve a statistician or data expert who can provide valuable input and guidance. Their expertise can help you navigate the complexities of data collection, ensure appropriate sampling techniques, and guide you in analyzing and interpreting the collected data accurately. Collaborating with a statistician enhances the rigor and validity of your evaluation process, leading to more robust and reliable findings.

## SURVEYS

Surveys are standardized written instruments administered by mail, e-mail, or in-person. The primary advantage of surveys is their cost in relation to the amount of data you can collect. Surveying is generally considered efficient because you can include large numbers of people at a relatively low cost. There are two key disadvantages to surveys. If a survey is conducted by mail, response rates can be meager, jeopardizing the validity of the data collected. There are mechanisms to increase response rates (i.e., gift cards, monetary rewards, transportation passes, and so on), but they will add to the cost of the survey. Written surveys also provide no opportunity for respondents to clarify a confusing question, again potentially creating a problem with the validity of responses. Good pre-testing of a survey instrument can reduce the likelihood of such issues arising. During a pre-test, your beta group will read your survey questions for interpretation, leading to clarity and consequent higher response reliability.

## INTERVIEWS AND FOCUS GROUPS

Interviews also use standardized instruments, but they are conducted person-to-person, either in-person or over the telephone. An interview may use the same instrument created for a written survey. However, interviewing generally provides the advantage of exploring questions more deeply than with a written survey. You can ask more complex questions in an interview since you can clarify any confusion. You also can ask respondents to elaborate on their answers, eliciting more in-depth information than a survey can provide. The primary disadvantage of interviews is their cost. It takes considerably more time and money to conduct telephone and in-person interviews. This usually means that you can collect information from far fewer people. The reliability of interviews can also be problematic if interviewers are not well-trained since they may ask questions in different ways or otherwise bias the responses.

While interviews with individuals are meant to solicit data without any influence or bias from the interviewer or other individuals, focus groups allow the participants to discuss the questions and share their opinions. This means people can influence one another, stimulating memory or debate on an issue. The advantage of focus groups lies in the richness of the information generated. The disadvantage is that you can rarely generalize or apply the findings to your entire population of participants or clients. Focus groups are often used before creating a survey to test concepts and wording of questions. Following a written survey, focus groups are used to explore specific questions or issues more thoroughly.

## OBSERVATION

Observations can be conducted on individual behaviors or interactions among individuals, events, or physical conditions within a site or facility. They require well-trained observers and detailed guidelines about whom or what to observe, when and for how long, and by what method of recording. The primary advantage of observation is its validity. When done well, observation is considered a robust data collection method because it generates first-hand, unbiased information by individuals who have been trained on what to look for and how to record it. However, observation requires time for development of the observation tool, training of the observers, and data collection, making it a more costly data collection method than some others.

## RECORD REVIEW

Record or document review involves systematically collecting data needed from internal, organizational, or official records collected by other groups or institutions. Internal records available to a capacity builder might include financial documents, monthly reports, activity logs, purchase orders, etc. The advantage of using records from your organization is the ease of data collection. The data is there, and no additional effort is required to collect it if the specific data you need is available and up to date. Record review is a very economical and efficient data collection method if the data is available. If the data you need is unavailable, it is likely well worth the time to make improvements to your data management system so that you can rely on internal record review for your outcome measurement requirements. Just a few changes to an existing form can turn it into a helpful data-collection tool. And just a small amount of staff training can increase the validity and reliability of internally generated data.

## SUMMARY OF COMMON RESEARCH METHODS

Note: this list is not exhaustive.

| Research Method | Research Design | Purpose | Example |
|---|---|---|---|
| Quantitative | Descriptive | To systematically describe an area of interest factually and accurately | Public opinion surveys |
| | Developmental | To investigate patterns of growth and/or change as a function of time | A trend study projecting the future growth and needs of a city water department |
| | Correlational | To investigate how variations in one factor correspond with variations in one or more other factors | A study to predict success in law school based on a learner's LSAT score |
| | Ex post facto | Investigate possible cause-and-effect relationships | Investigate differences between groups, such as smokers and non-smokers |
| | True experi-mental | Investigate possible cause-and-effect relationships between treatment groups and control groups | Investigate the effects of HIV on patients using AZT and a control group of AIDS patients using a placebo |
| | Quasi-experi-mental | Approximate the conduct of a true experiment | An attempt to get casual factors in real-life settings where only actual control is possible |
| Qualitative | Case study | Seeks to uncover the interplay of significant factors characteristic of a phenomena | The importance of setting in adult education programs |
| | Historical | Goes back to past events and people to examine the early building blocks of the field in order to illuminate present practice | Study of vocational education |
| | Ethnographic | Study of human society and culture | An anthropologist's study of a culture |

| | | | |
|---|---|---|---|
| Qualitative | Grounded theory | Characterized by inductive fieldwork and the building of theory | Continuing professional education for CPAs |
| | Critical | Knowledge ¾ Constitutive interests | Education as a social project in South Central Los Angeles |
| | Futures | Emphasize the importance of the past to illuminate the future | The next two or three decades and beyond in computer sciences |
| | Phenomenon – logical | Seeks to deepen our level of consciousness and broaden our range of experiences | Study of the theoretical basis for the practice of matrix organizations |
| | Action Rese-arch | Develop new skills to solve problems with direct application | An in-service training program to help managers develop new skills on the Internet |
| | Field study | Intensive study of background, status, and environmental interaction of a given social unit | The best way to teach adults job survival skills |
| | Participatory | Research that has empowerment and human equality as its aim | Development of a curriculum in Miami, Florida, for teaching English in the workplace |
| Evaluative | Cost-benefit analysis | Used to determine if programs currently in operation are producing benefits that justify their costs | A study to make sound decisions on allocating personnel and budget at a state university |
| | Needs analysis | Procedure of identifying and prioritizing needs related to societal, organizational, and human performance | Assessment of the information systems for the state of Arizona |

**Note: this list is not exhaustive.**

| Research Method | Research Design | Purpose | Example |
|---|---|---|---|
| Quantitative | Descriptive | To systematically describe an area of interest factually and accurately | Public opinion surveys |
| | Developmental | To investigate patterns of growth and/or change as a function of time | A trend study projecting the future growth and needs of a city water department |
| | Correlational | To investigate how variations in one factor correspond with variations in one or more other factors | A study to predict success in law school based on a learner's LSAT score |
| | Ex post facto | Investigate possible cause-and-effect relationships | Investigate differences between groups, such as smokers and non-smokers |
| | True experi-mental | Investigate possible cause-and-effect relationships between treatment groups and control groups | Investigate the effects of HIV on patients using AZT and a control group of AIDS patients using a placebo |
| | Quasi-experi-mental | Approximate the conduct of a true experiment | An attempt to get casual factors in real-life settings where only actual control is possible |
| Qualitative | Case study | Seeks to uncover the interplay of significant factors characteristic of a phenomena | The importance of setting in adult education programs |
| | Historical | Goes back to past events and people to examine the early building blocks of the field in order to illuminate present practice | Study of vocational education |

| | | | |
|---|---|---|---|
| Qualitative | Ethnographic | Study of human society and culture | An anthropologist's study of a culture |
| | Grounded theory | Characterized by inductive fieldwork and the building of theory | Continuing professional education for CPAs |
| | Critical | Knowledge ¾ Constitutive interests | Education as a social project in South Central Los Angeles |
| | Futures | Emphasize the importance of the past to illuminate the future | The next two or three decades and beyond in computer sciences |
| | Phenomenon – logical | Seeks to deepen our level of consciousness and broaden our range of experiences | Study of the theoretical basis for the practice of matrix organizations |
| | Action Rese-arch | Develop new skills to solve problems with direct application | An in-service training program to help managers develop new skills on the Internet |
| | Field study | Intensive study of background, status, and environmental interaction of a given social unit | The best way to teach adults job survival skills |
| | Participatory | Research that has empowerment and human equality as its aim | Development of a curriculum in Miami, Florida for teaching English in the workplace |
| Evaluative | Cost-benefit analysis | Used to determine if programs currently in operation are producing benefits that justify their costs | A study to make sound decisions on allocating personnel and budget at a state university |
| | Needs analysis | Procedure of identifying and prioritizing needs related to societal, organizational, and human performance | Assessment of the information systems for the state of Arizona |

## EXERCISE 7.2: CHECKLIST FOR CHOOSING DATA COLLECTION METHOD

This checklist can help you decide which data collection methods are most appropriate for your outcome measurement.[1]

| Surveys | | |
|---|---|---|
| **1. Do I need data from the perspective of the participant, client, beneficiary, or customer?** | Yes | No |
| **2. Do I have a systemic way to get it from these individuals?** | Yes | No |
| **3. Do I need standardized data so that statistical comparisons can be made?** | Yes | No |
| **4. Will participants be able to understand the survey question?[1]** | Yes | No |
| **5. Do participants have the knowledge or awareness to answer questions about the outcomes accurately?** | Yes | No |
| ***If you answered Yes to questions 1 through 5, surveys might be appropriate for collecting data on your outcomes and indicators.*** | | |

| Interviews | | |
|---|---|---|
| **1. Are more in-depth answers necessary to adequately measure the indicators or get information on what is needed or should change?** | Yes | No |
| **2. Will it be necessary for someone to personally ask participants questions to collect the information related to this outcome?** | Yes | No |
| ***If you answered Yes to questions 1 and 2, interviews might be appropriate for collecting data on your outcomes and indicators.*** | | |

| Observation | | |
|---|---|---|
| **1. Is it difficult to accurately measure the indicators by asking people questions about opinions or perceptions?** | Yes | No |
| **2. Can this outcome or indicator be assessed accurately by someone trained to observe it in action?** | Yes | No |
| **3. Do you have the staff resources for someone to observe events, conditions, interactions, or behaviors?** | Yes | No |
| ***If you answered Yes to questions 1 through 3, observation may be appropriate for collecting data on your outcomes and indicators.*** | | |

1 When designing a survey, you want to do a pilot study where individuals review the questions of your survey and provide feedback on their design.

| Internal Record Review | | |
|---|---|---|
| 1. Do you have individualized records, reports, logs, or other systematic ways that you track things in your program or services? | Yes | No |
| 2. If an information system exists, is the data consistently entered into it in a timely way? | Yes | No |
| 3. If a system exists, can information be extracted from it quickly? | Yes | No |
| *If you answered Yes to questions 1 through 3, an internal record review might be appropriate for collecting data on your outcomes and indicators.* | | |

| Official Record Review | | |
|---|---|---|
| 1. Do official records exist that track the data you need on your outcomes and indicators? | Yes | No |
| 2. Are the data accessible to you? | Yes | No |
| *If you answered Yes to questions 1 and 2, an official record review might be appropriate for collecting data on your outcomes and indicators.* | | |

## POPULATION AND SAMPLE OR SOURCE OF DATA

It would be best if you described the subjects of your data collection activity. For some, this will include a description of the people sampled and how they were contacted. You should describe your role and the roles of any assistants or field workers in conducting the study. The uses and characteristics of any subjects should also be described. You should focus on characteristics that affected the outcome of the study (age, experience, training, etc.) and present data in tables, if appropriate. You should provide information on how they assured that subjects were treated ethically. Other studies may not incorporate people. The subjects may be products or an assembly line. Any element which comprises the data can be considered a subject.

## WAYS TO FAIL

So what could go wrong with your data collection design that would make a reviewer believe the grant could fail? First, there could be a misalignment between the study population or design and the study's objectives. Second, there would be insufficient time for recruitment and follow-up. This also tends to happen when a nonprofit is new to grant applications and does not understand the importance this section can have on the outcome of the application process. There could also be a lack of clarity concerning the availability of subjects. Lastly, if technical details are too standard, they can be uninteresting.

## SUMMARY

Defining outcomes and selecting appropriate indicators are crucial steps in program evaluation. As a capacity-building organization, it is important to focus on the impacts or changes your program or service brings to the client organization, rather than simply describing activities. Select a few key outcomes directly connected to your assistance and develop clear and measurable outcome statements. Ensure that outcome or performance indicators are specific and observable, answering questions about how changes will be recognized and achieved. Consider various data collection methods, such as surveys, interviews, observation, and record review, and weigh their advantages and disadvantages in terms of the information needed, validity and reliability, available resources, and cultural appropriateness. Involving a statistician or data expert can provide valuable input and guidance to enhance the rigor and validity of data collection and analysis.

To ensure effective data collection, carefully consider the alignment between outcomes and indicators, select specific and observable indicators, and choose appropriate data collection methods. Involve a statistician or data expert to enhance the validity and reliability of your evaluation. Additionally, be mindful of potential pitfalls, including misalignment between study population and objectives, insufficient time for recruitment and follow-up, lack of clarity regarding subject availability, and uninteresting technical details. By following these guidelines, you can develop a well-designed data collection plan that accurately measures outcomes and supports your program evaluation efforts.

# CHAPTER EIGHT
## Sustainability

All federal and state agencies require grant writers to describe their sustainability plans. Some foundations will also request this information but not all. It is good practice to think about sustainability whether it is requested or not, and include this in your application. The sustainability plan is often the most challenging piece of the proposal to write and can be a considerable hurdle to completing the submission. However, strategies are available for systematically designing and presenting the sustainability plan, including using data obtained from the project; aligning the targeted audience with the Request for Proposal, developing detailed descriptions of services and activities post-funding; identifying key staff needed to manage future programming; involving key stakeholders in identifying strategies; and finding champions for your cause.

**Why do funders place such great importance on program sustainability?**

Consider that introducing a new endeavor (program) may have high visibility for a short period but fail to be sustainable after initial efforts. If this happens, a sense of resentment within local communities is likely. Communities may become wary of participating in other opportunities in the future if it is perceived that these, too, may be short-lived. The possibility of this result alone is reason to require grantees to document sustainability beyond funding life, even though it can be challenging. Even if the grant recipient does everything right and has an exemplary program, keep in mind that as worthy as a project or program may be, it will not sustain itself. Careful long term vision and planning followed by systematically undertaking the appropriate steps to maintain it, is required.

**How can you build sustainability into your program?**

One of the most common proposed solutions to state is that 'we will continue to look for other grants to sustain our program'. However, this volatility does not make a funder feel secure in the program's ability to continue beyond the funding end date. Funders consider themselves social entrepreneurs and want to invest their funds into programs that will continue beyond their funding. They will look for the best match with the least amount of risk. At the same time, while most of a nonprofit's funding comes from donations and grants, you also need to consider other ways to generate revenue. We can discuss these revenue streams in our grant applications, but it is best to demonstrate different ways that concretely show sustainability. As for-profit organizations, you should aim to create as much diversity in your revenue stream as possible. Many creative examples are available. Below are some ideas on how to build sustainability into your program:

- **Fee for Service** – While many nonprofits cringe at this idea, we need to remember that this is a business that needs to be managed as such. Many people can afford to pay something for the service they are receiving. This can be a flat or a sliding fee based on individual income.
- **Membership Program** – Is there a way to charge a membership fee for your service? This can

be a flat or a sliding fee based on individual income.

- **Corporate Sponsorships** – Can your nonprofit connect with local for-profit organizations to sponsor your nonprofit? It is an excellent social responsibility for the for-profit organization and provides a revenue stream for your nonprofit.

## EXERCISE 8.1: SUSTAINABILITY EXERCISE

Thinking about sustainability is not something that should be left until your grant comes to an end. You will need time to think about the following, starting before your grant application:

**Identify short-term and long-term sustainability strategies that will work for your organization.**

____________________________________________________________

____________________________________________________________

____________________________________________________________

____________________________________________________________

____________________________________________________________

**Identify resources needed to sustain your project (e.g., faculty, staff, equipment, space, etc.) and work toward obtaining them.**

____________________________________________________________

____________________________________________________________

____________________________________________________________

____________________________________________________________

____________________________________________________________

**Establish a formal or informal group to address sustainability. Who will be part of this group and why?**

Name: ____________________________________________________

Role: _____________________________________________________

Strengths to the Group: ________________________________________

____________________________________________________________

Name: ____________________

Role: ____________________

Strengths to the Group: ____________________

____________________

Name: ____________________

Role: ____________________

Strengths to the Group: ____________________

____________________

Name: ____________________

Role: ____________________

Strengths to the Group: ____________________

____________________

Name: ____________________

Role: ____________________

Strengths to the Group: ____________________

____________________

Name: ____________________

Role: ____________________

Strengths to the Group: ____________________

____________________

Name: ____________________

Role: ____________________

Strengths to the Group: ____________________

______________________________________________________________

Develop action steps for your sustainability plan: ______________________________

______________________________________________________________

## SUSTAINABILITY TIPS

- **Take Sustainability seriously** - Don't assume that if the idea is good, it will automatically attract future support. Sustainability must be planned.
- **Set clear and realistic expectations** – What do you hope to sustain? What makes the most sense?
- **Collaborate with partners** – on an ongoing basis. Make sure your partners realize the benefit of participating in your project, are kept up to date on how the project is doing, and feel involved. Build a role for partners to participate in developing and implementing the sustainability plan, into the project design.
- **Document and evaluate outputs and outcomes as marketing tools** – Produce data and reports that can be used to explain the initiative's mission and successes and serve as outreach tools to garner further support. Toot your own horn as you go along. Don't wait until the end of the grant to get the word out about your successes.

## SUMMARY

A sustainability plan is critical to funders because they want to ensure that the grant impact will continue beyond the terms of funding. This can be seen as similar to start-up funding for a for-profit. Some things that can be focused on are the designation of staff, future marketing for the cause and fundraising plans along with track record, board of director pledges available upon request, fee-for-service projections, and so on.

# CHAPTER NINE
# Budget and Budget Narratives/Justifications

The budget and budget narratives are an essential aspect of your grant submission. Often, funders will look at the budget aspects first to determine the reality of your ask and if you have a good sense of the numbers. This will also give a potential funder some insight into the financial knowledge of an organization. Potential funders will also look at the narrative to explain any variances in the numbers from year to year. When developing your budget and budget narrative, you want to include someone from your organization's finance department. Without this support from the finance department, it is easy to misallocate expenses on your budget, leading to cost overruns when the grant is awarded. You want to avoid this at all costs. Additionally, if good internal financial policies are in place, you will need financial information for your budget that a grant writer will not have access to.

## BUDGET NARRATIVES

Also known as a budget detail, budget description, or budget justification, the budget narrative explains the nature of the numbers, i.e., what the budget table or spreadsheet numbers represent and how you arrived at them. The narrative will document every number in your budget. It should be a written mirror image and explain any variances in the numbers. The benefit of preparing a budget narrative is that it requires you to get down to your project's nitty-gritty details by laying out how you arrived at costs for accomplishing what and when. Along with the budget, the budget narrative tells a funder exactly how a nonprofit will spend its investment, item by item. From a funder's perspective, the budget narrative ensures:

- You researched, and your project costs are reasonable and well thought out.
- Your project is within the funder's giving range, and/or it includes a plan to seek additional funding.

## WHEN TO START WRITING

Since many of your budget calculations must be explained in the budget narrative, you can simultaneously save time by writing your budget and budget narrative. The sooner you start it, the better. This should be one of the first documents your write, and you should include someone from your nonprofit with financial experience. Of course, some project planning work needs to happen first, but the sooner you start looking at the resources you will need and begin pricing them out, the faster your project will move from the realm of ideas into reality.

## BASIC COST CATEGORIES

Most government agencies put constraints on what can be included in the budget and on the maximum amounts that can be requested, for example, for indirect costs. Some federal proposals ask for a very detailed budget narrative, requiring you to break out the budget narrative by project activity, discuss cost-per-participant, and explain how administrative (indirect) costs support project goals. Foundations are typically less prescriptive. However, for both public and private sector grants, the budget narrative should state clearly and concisely where the amounts in each budget category will come from and what they will cover. All expenses should relate clearly to the project narrative. Additionally, the budget narrative should show clearly which budget items will be covered by matching funds or leveraged resources. Your budget narrative should detail the following:

- **Personnel** – Include the hours, wages, and duties of each grant-related position.
- **Fringe benefits** – List all employment-related costs, such as FICA, worker's compensation, health insurance, retirement benefits, etc.
- **Travel** – Cover mileage, airline tickets, taxis, car rentals, mileage reimbursements, parking fees, tolls, tips, per diems for lodging and meals, etc.
- **Contracts** – Specify contract services, such as leases, consultants' fees, training, etc.
- **Major and Minor Equipment** – List all purchases for items with a life span of (usually) three years or more, such as furniture, computers, copy/fax machines, lab equipment, telephones, software, etc.
- **Materials/Supplies** – Include short-lived items needed to run an office, such as paper, envelopes, pens and pencils, CDs, staples, etc.
- **Capital Expenses** – Include the purchase and/or construction and renovation of land, buildings, accompanying fixtures, etc.

Regardless of the funder's requirements, presenting a detailed budget and budget narrative is good practice. Even if it is only for internal purposes. It is very easy to underestimate the program's or service's actual costs when you do not take the time to compile a proper budget and budget narrative. A funder will detect this during their review. Many nonprofits do not take the time to do this because it is time-consuming. However, extra time during the planning stage can save you from many headaches later.

## EXERCISE 9.1: KEY-PERSONNEL EXERCISE

When identifying personnel, you want to categorize individuals as either key or non-key personnel. Key personnel are individuals who bring a unique skill set to the grant. If key personnel were to leave during the duration of the grant, it would cause a delay in the progress of the program or service while you replace that individual. Non-key personnel are individuals who would not cause this delay, such as research assistants.

1. **Identify a Project Administrator** - This person will oversee the project. They will be responsible for evaluating whether or not grant objectives are being met to help prepare for evaluation. The Administrator needs to allocate at least five hours per week to ensure they meet the funders' conditions.

2. **Identify a Project Director**-This person will be responsible for project implementation and carrying out tasks on a day-to-day basis. The Director will report to the Administrator, and they must be very knowledgeable and skilled in the same subjects as the project. Make a quick list of the qualifications for each position to work on your grant project. Do not attach a name or try to think of a specific person. Only think about the characteristics of your ideally qualified person.

**Project Administrator**

1.
2.
3.
4.
5.

**Project Director**

1.
2.
3.
4.
5.

## UNUSUAL EXPENDITURES

If the project is small, costs are normally straightforward, and the numbers tell the story. While the funder may not require a budget narrative, completing one is still good practice. If your budget contains any unusual items, use your budget narrative to explain them to the funder, even if they do not request one. For example, a fire and safety proposal budget that includes a purchase of *Pluggie*, the talking fire hydrant, will benefit from a budget narrative that explains: *Pluggie* is a tool for the Fire Prevention Team to use in teaching fire safety. Operated by remote control, *Pluggie* moves, speaks and plays cassettes. Team members will use *Pluggie* in working on elementary school presentations. This thoroughness shows the funder that your project team has thought through all its proposed expenditures.

## BUDGET NARRATIVE STRUCTURE

Most federal proposals explain how to structure the budget narrative. However, private and corporate funders often leave this decision up to you. For simple projects, one option is to incorporate the budget narrative into the budget by inserting a brief explanation under each item. In this case, the budget narrative may be included on a spreadsheet.

Another option is to number items in the left margin or attach footnote-style numbers to each line and follow the numeric budget with Notes to the Budget where in each numbered item can then be explained. Regardless of the format, the categories in the narrative should use budget headings, following the exact order in which the items are listed in the numerical budget, and include semi-totals.

Below are examples of how some categories in a budget narrative can be compiled. APPENDIX III has a complete budget narrative template for you to refer to. First, a word about abbreviations - don't be afraid to use them, especially when it is essential to conserve space. Mathematical symbols and equations can also be a part of a budget narrative. The guiding rule to follow is clarity.

**A. Personnel** – List each position that pertains to the proposal. The cost calculation should show the employee's annual salary rate and the percentage of time devoted to the project. Compensation for employees engaged in grant activities should be consistent with that paid for similar work within the organization.

1. Project Director: $35,000/year @ 100% = $35,000. The Project Director oversees the program and will spend 100% of her time hiring, training, and supervising staff. Grant funds will cover this individual's annual salary for the 12 months of the contract.

2. Two School Safety Officers: 2 x $35.00/hour x 3 hours/day x 5 days/month x 12 months. (Covered by matching funds.)

**B. Fringe** – Fringe benefits are based on the applicant's established formula and are only for the percentage of time devoted to the project. It is essential to explain what is included in the benefits package and at what percentage.

1. Director: $65,000 x 18.55% = $11,115. A request of $6,493 will cover the fringe benefits for the Director at a rate of 18.55%. Benefits include FICA @ 6.2%, Health/Life insurance @ 8.9%, and Workers comp @ 2.0%.

2. Assistant Director: $45,000 x 18.55% x .25 = 2086.88. (A breakdown of the fringe rate is included in the Budget Detail Worksheet.)

**C. Staff Development** – This may include required or desired training, workshops, or classes for staff. The project-related purpose should be highlighted.

1. The Program Assistant will attend continuing education classes at the local community college in the area of social work and administration for two semesters to ensure state-of-the-art wraparound case management. 2 semesters x 2 classes x $275.00/class = $1,100.00.

**D. Travel**[1] – Explain the reason for travel expenses for project personnel (e.g., staff to training, field interviews, advisory group meeting, etc.) and show the number of trainees and unit costs involved. Identify the location of travel.

1. Regional/Statewide Meeting: Three people to funder-required three-day training in Destination City.

- 3 people x $500 airfare = $1,500
- 3 people x 3 days x $40 per diem = $360
- 3 people x 2 nights x $100.00 hotel = $600

**E. Minor Equipment**[2] - List non-expendable items to be purchased. Explain how the equipment is necessary for the project's success and, if requested, the procurement method to be used. The organization's capitalization policy for equipment can be used unless the funder provides one to follow.

- One computer package will be purchased, including a laptop, printer, scanner, and Word Programs. The computer will be housed in the administrative office and checked out by staff when they go out into the field. It will be networked into the office network to maintain client databases and perform administrative work connected to the project.

---

1 Travel always has to be done on a domestic carrier and only coach level fairs are reimbursable.

2 A budget can have major and minor equipment. If one unit is less than $5k it is minor equipment and if one unit is over $5k is it major equipment. Major equipment cannot be included in the indirect calculations

**F. Supplies**[3] - List expendable items by type and show the basis for computation.

1. Meeting Supplies: For administrative meetings, workshops, etc., $75.00 x 12 months = $900.00.

**G. Consultants**[4] - Describe the product or services to be provided by the consultant and an estimate or detailing of exact costs. Indicate the applicant's formal, written procurement policy unless asked to follow a different policy. Include a) Consultant Fees (for each consultant, enter the name, service, hourly or daily fee, and estimated time on the project) and b) Consultant Expenses (list all expenses to be paid from the grant to the individual consultant in addition to their fees, such as travel, meals, lodging, etc.).

1. The Computer Instructor will conduct four computer-training sessions weekly in the computer lab. The Community Outreach Trainer will develop a curriculum for Community Outreach and train neighborhood associations on the curriculum. The 2.5 FTE Tutors will tutor children at the after school.

- Computer Instructor: $11.10/hour x 26 hours/week x 52 weeks = $15,000

**I. Administrative or Indirect Costs** – Some funders allow for indirect costs, which represent the expenses of doing business that are not directly tied to a particular project function or activity. Indirect cost rates distribute those costs among all the work that the nonprofit engages in. If allowed for, a funder will typically specify the percentage of the total requested amount which may be allocated toward indirect or administrative costs. This is usually around 8 - 15%.

Funders use these factors to assess budgets:

- Can the job be accomplished with this budget?
- Are costs reasonable for the market - or too high or low?
- Is the budget consistent with the proposed activities?
- Is there sufficient budget detail and explanation?

**I. Administrative or Indirect Costs** – Some funders allow for indirect costs, which represent the expenses of doing business that are not directly tied to a particular project function or activity. Indirect cost rates distribute those costs among all the work that the nonprofit engages in. If allowed for, a funder will typically specify the percentage of the total requested amount which may be allocated toward indirect or administrative costs. This is usually around 8 - 15%.

**Funders use these factors to assess budgets:**

- Can the job be accomplished with this budget?
- Are costs reasonable for the market - or too high or low?
- Is the budget consistent with the proposed activities?
- Is there sufficient budget detail and explanation?

3 Office supplies cannot be charged to a grant. These costs are covered through the indirect dollars.

4 It is critical to be certain about your consultant designation. The IRS says someone cannot be classified as a consultant if your organization has that position in-house. You can still use the individual but they need to be classified as a temporary employee which has social security benefits applied to them.

## EXERCISE 9.2: BUDGET PLANNING EXERCISE

List all the expenditures for your project:

_______________________________________________

_______________________________________________

_______________________________________________

_______________________________________________

_______________________________________________

We have just detailed all of the expenditures for your project. But what about the income? Projected income on a project could make your proposal more attractive to funders (remember sustainability). Here are some examples of possible income:

- Membership fees
- Ticket sales (This could apply to a grant for performing arts.)
- Special events (Are you planning any additional fundraisers?)
- Other funders (Any additional interest from other funders or interest earned on an endowment?)
- Tuition

List all the revenue streams for your project:

_______________________________________________

_______________________________________________

_______________________________________________

_______________________________________________

_______________________________________________

## COMMON BUDGETING MISTAKES

**Appendix II** has a complete budget template which would be good to refer to for compiling a detailed budget and budget requirements. Remember, including someone from your finance department when preparing your budget is always good practice. A mistake in allocating costs early on can be extremely after the grant is awarded. Below are some common budgeting mistakes:

- Employees vs. Independent contractors
  • A contractor is an individual outside your organization performing a task that no one in your organization currently does. In the case that you use someone outside your organization, but someone in your organization can do the job, the individual has to be categorized as a temporary

employee, and your nonprofit has to pay social security for that individual. This could result in a cost overrun if not budgeted correctly.

- **Paying Participants**
  • If you choose to pay a participant in your study, the total budget for these payments must be excluded from your indirect costs. You are not allowed to include this as indirect costs.

- **Travel**
  • There are a lot of foreign travel restrictions. Individuals cannot get reimbursed for a foreign carrier. They always need to fly on a domestic carrier. Individuals can only be reimbursed for a coach fair. Often travelling personnel will need to front travel costs because it cannot be charged to the grant until after the travel has taken place.

Regardless of the type of grant you are applying for, it is best to put good post-award management into place. The federal government provides some excellent guidelines through its OMB circulars. Many of these should be followed to ensure good practices before compiling your budget, you can educate yourself on what should be included or avoided ahead of time to not make the mistakes later. The OMB Circular A-110 covers Institutions of Higher Education, Hospitals, and other Non-profit Organizations. Below are some A-110 highlights:

## OMB Circular A-110 Highlights

- Establishes prior approval requirements
  - change in scope
  - change in key personnel
  - absence of PI for more than three months or a 25% reduction in time
  - need for additional federal funding
  - transfer direct/indirect costs
  - costs requiring approval per A-21
  - transfer of trainee stipends to other categories
  - sub awards unless approved in prime award
- Agencies can authorize the following (these "expanded authorities" automatic for research)
  - ninety-day pre-award costs
  - one-time no-cost extension
  - carryforward of unobligated balances
- Agencies may require approval for transfer among budget categories (10%)
- Requires positive efforts to utilize small and small disadvantaged businesses
- Requires cost & price analysis on every procurement
- Record retention requirements
  - three years after submission of the final expenditure report or audit, whichever is later
  - can be electronic (approved through the cognizant agency)
  - allows federal access to records
  - F&A & other cost allocation plans also in three year period
  - technical records are included
- Requires managing & monitoring of financial & program performance, including sub-awards
- Performance reports are required not more often than quarterly but at least once annually

- Prescribes contents of performance reports
- Requires financial reports and describes the content
- Reports due within ninety calendar days of award termination
- Prescribes closeout procedures
    - reports are due 90 calendar days after completion
        - financial
        - performance
        - other
- Requires refunds of unobligated balances

When preparing a budget, think twice before allocating 100% of any cost to a grant. Ask yourself the following question:

CAN YOU GUARANTEE THE ITEM WILL **NEVER** BE USED FOR ANYTHING OTHER THAN THE GRANT?

The answer to this question is very seldom YES! When you charge something 100% to a grant, it will be a yellow or red flag during an audit. If that is the case, you need to have a good rationale for it. For example, if you charge 100% of a laptop purchase to a grant, can you guarantee that no one will ever check their email, look something up on the Internet that is not grant-related, or engage in any unrelated other activities? It is impossible to ensure this. Therefore it is best to only charge 95% of the cost to the grant. This guideline holds true for any grant expense.

## SUMMARY

The budget and budget narratives are crucial components of a grant submission, as they provide funders with insight into the financial knowledge of an organization and help determine the feasibility of the funding request. When developing the budget and budget narrative, it is essential to involve someone from the organization's finance department to ensure accurate allocation of expenses and avoid cost overruns. Good internal financial policies and information from the finance department are necessary for creating a comprehensive and well-thought-out budget.

The budget narrative, also known as a budget detail or budget justification, explains the nature of the numbers in the budget and provides a detailed breakdown of each expense. It helps funders understand the reasoning behind the budget figures and any variances from year to year. The budget narrative should clearly state where the amounts in each budget category will come from and what they will cover, ensuring transparency and demonstrating that costs have been thoroughly researched and considered. Additionally, the budget narrative should explain any unusual expenditures and provide a comprehensive overview of how the nonprofit will spend the funding.

Writing the budget and budget narrative should be initiated early in the grant application process, and the budget calculations should be simultaneously explained in the narrative. By starting early, organizations can accurately determine the resources needed and their associated costs, helping move the project from ideation to reality. The budget narrative should include key cost categories such as personnel, fringe benefits, travel, contracts, major and minor equipment, materials/supplies, and capital expenses. Regardless of the funder's requirements, presenting a detailed budget and budget narrative is essential to avoid underestimating costs and ensure a successful grant application.

# CHAPTER TEN
## Final Steps to Submission

Now that you have completed writing your grant, you want to ensure you spent ample time editing it. A funder will see small mistakes as a lack of attention to detail and will wonder if this lack of detail will also transfer to your program or service. Hiring someone to review and edit your proposal is never a bad idea. An outside perspective will not only help to catch small mistakes but also expose any unclear or incomplete sections. Below is a checklist you can use for some of the major items:

### GRANT WRITING CHECKLIST

| ITEM | Completed |
|---|---|
| Did we assume that the reader is stupid? | ☐ |
| Did we speak the funder's language? | ☐ |
| Did we follow directions? | ☐ |
| Do we have a good elevator pitch? | ☐ |
| Did we create and follow our logic model? | ☐ |
| Did we work ahead/Do we have a previous RFP? | ☐ |
| Do we have measurable outcomes? | ☐ |
| Did we establish alignment between the funder's goals and our program's goals? | ☐ |
| Did we create continuity throughout each section of the grant? | ☐ |

A final review by others is also a great idea. You should try and get as many people as possible to review the grant. This should include individuals who know about your grant and those who don't know anything about it. The rubric below is an excellent tool for scoring your grant proposal

| | EXEMPLARY (3 PTS) | ADEQUATE (2 PTS) | NEEDS IMPROVEMENT (1 PT) | MISSING (0 PTS) | SCORE | COMMENTS |
|---|---|---|---|---|---|---|
| Introduction & Literature Review | Provides a clear and thorough introduction and background | Provides an introduction and background that is only somewhat significant to the experiment | Provides an introduction and background that is insignificant to the experiment | Introduction and/or background not provided | | |
| Purpose and Objectives | States a specific testable research question | States a clear, but untestable research question | States a vague, untestable research question | No research question posed | | |
| Methodology | Provides a clear explanation of the proposed experimental methods | Provides an adequate explanation of proposed experimental methods | Provides and unorganized explanation of experimental methods | Explanation of experimental methods missing | | |
| Justification | Presents rationale and significance of proposed work in the form of a well-structured, logical argument | Shows some effort to present the rationale and significance of proposed work in the form of a well-structured argument | Presents rationale and significance of proposed work in the form of a weak, unstructured argument | rationale and significance of proposed work not articulated | | |
| Writing Technique | Uses acceptable style and grammar (0 errors) | Uses adequate style and grammar (1-2 errors) | Fails to use acceptable style and grammar (2-5 errors) | Serious style and grammar flaws (>5 errors) | | |
| Argument Structure | Provides strong, clear, convincing conclusions why the proposed method should be used and evidence, i.e. relevant examples to support the conclusions | Provides conclusions explaining why the proposed method should be used, but weak evidence, i.e. no specific (only generalized) examples to support the conclusions | Provides conclusions explaining why the proposed method should be used but no concrete evidence in the form of examples | No conclusions articulated explaining why the proposed method should be used | | |
| Feasibility | The equipment is available and the timeline appropriate for conducting the proposed experiment | The equipment is available but the timeline is inappropriate for conducting the proposed experiment | | Neither the equipment nor the timeline are appropriate for conducting the experiment | | |

**GOOD LUCK WITH YOUR GRANT SUBMISSION!!!**

# CHAPTER ELEVEN
## Post-Award Management

Congratulations! If you have made it this far, your organization has either been awarded a grant or is anticipating a grant award. This is no small feat! While writing the grant proposal was hard work, the implementation of the grant is now beginning. The post-award management of the grant has officially started. What exactly does that mean?

*Post-award management is implementing sponsor policies and procedures. Sound management of sponsored programs is critical in maintaining public trust.*

First, notify the relevant people. Your staff needs to be notified of the grant and when it begins so they can plan staffing, expansion, and layout timelines. Additionally, your accounting/finance staff must take over the financial management. A temporarily restricted fund should be set up in your chart of accounts where all grant expenses will be booked. This will help with active monitoring, which can alternatively be accomplished through a review of reports, correspondence from the grantee, audit reports, and site visits.

Active Monitoring plays a crucial role in managing funder expectations within a project plan, particularly when it comes to grants. Grants are a common form of funding for projects, and they often come with specific requirements and expectations from the funding organization. By actively monitoring the project's progress and aligning it with funder expectations, project managers can ensure that they are prepared for review and progress reports, avoiding unpleasant surprises and maintaining a positive relationship with the funders.

To effectively manage funder expectations within your project plan, consider the following forms that active monitoring can take on in the context of grants:

1. **Proposal Compliance:** Active monitoring begins right from the proposal stage. Thoroughly review the grant guidelines and requirements to ensure that your proposal complies with all the necessary criteria. By actively monitoring the proposal's alignment with the funder's objectives and guidelines, you can increase your chances of success and set the foundation for managing funder expectations throughout the project.
2. **Project Timeline and Milestones:** Clearly define the project timeline and establish milestones that align with the grant's objectives. Actively monitor and track progress against these milestones to ensure that the project stays on schedule. By regularly updating funders on milestone achievements, you can demonstrate progress and manage their expectations regarding the project's timeline.
3. **Budget Utilization:** Grants often come with specific budget allocations and restrictions. Actively monitor the project's budget utilization and ensure that it aligns with the grant's guidelines. Regularly track expenses, review financial reports, and communicate any significant deviations from the original budget to the funders. Proactive management of the budget helps set realistic expectations and avoids surprises during financial reviews.

4. **Regular Communication**: Establish a communication plan with the funding organization to maintain an ongoing dialogue. Schedule regular check-ins and progress updates to discuss the project's status, challenges, and achievements. These interactions provide an opportunity to actively monitor funder expectations, address any concerns, and align project activities with their priorities. Keeping funders informed fosters transparency and reduces the likelihood of surprises during review or progress reports.
5. **Impact Assessment**: Many grants require projects to demonstrate their impact or outcomes. Actively monitor and assess the project's progress towards achieving the intended impact. Define and measure key performance indicators (KPIs) that reflect the grant's goals and regularly report on the progress made. By actively monitoring the project's impact, you can manage funder expectations and provide evidence of the project's success.
6. **Risk Management**: Actively identify and manage risks throughout the project lifecycle. Regularly assess potential risks and implement mitigation strategies to minimize their impact. By actively monitoring and addressing risks, you can demonstrate to funders that you are proactive in ensuring project success and managing unexpected challenges. Communicating your risk management efforts helps build trust and manage funder expectations regarding project uncertainties.

By incorporating these forms of active monitoring into your project plan, you can effectively manage funder expectations within the context of grants. Being well-prepared for review and progress reports is crucial, as it maintains a positive relationship with the funding organization and increases the likelihood of continued support. Active monitoring not only helps you meet funder expectations but also enables you to identify and address any deviations or challenges promptly, increasing the overall success of the project.

There are a few other things to consider when setting up the post-award management of the grant:

- **Payroll** – The personnel on the budget should be reviewed, and their salary will need to be reallocated so the correct percentage will be charged to the grant. This should be checked twice a year with the program manager to ensure it is accurate, and personnel action reports (PARs) should be signed off on and stored.
- **Consultants** – If the grant budget provides for any consultants, they should be contacted and notified of the grant reward. It is critical to ensure that these individuals meet the federal guidelines to perform services as a consultant. A consultant is conducting work that the nonprofit would not typically conduct. However, if that is not the case, they will need to be set up as temporary employees. The difference is that a consultant will bill for services, and the grant will pay them directly, delivering a W-9 at the end of the fiscal year. However, if they are a temporary employee, they will receive a paycheck, with social security benefits taken out of it. Let's look at a closer example because it can be confusing to determine which status is correct. If your nonprofit is an educational institute and you employ statisticians, then an external statistician could not serve as a consultant. They would need to be set up as a temporary employee.
- **Subcontracts** – A subcontract is when another organization will conduct a portion of the grant work. If the grant budget provides for a subcontract, the organization needs to be notified, and a contract needs to be put into place. They will be required to provide billing and reports based on the terms laid out in the grant agreement. The contract must meet the funder's requirements, but the subcontractee can add additional terms and conditions.

It is important to get your financial system set up immediately so, tracking can begin. It is essential to conduct monthly reviews of all expenditures charged to the grant. This way, an error is caught early and can be corrected through a journal entry. A complete internal audit of all the grants should be conducted yearly to ensure nothing is missed.

## COST PRINCIPLES

The cost principles for grants are (1) allowable, (2) allocable, (3) reasonable, and (4) consistent. These are the guiding principles for applying grant expenses and supporting sound business practices. One needs to ask themselves if the cost is necessary and reasonable. It is essential to ensure that bidding takes place before selecting a vendor, as expenses must be comparable to market value. Once the expense is ready to be charged, it must be allocable. Can it be charged 100% to the grant? There are very few cases where the answer to this question is yes. When booking any expense, you must determine what other funds are applicable and the percentage breakdown for each. This will also ensure you are compliant with any grant spending laws. Lastly, how you charge grant expenses needs to be consistent. For example, if someone's salary is allocated at 25% of their base, it must be consistently charged that way every month. The percentages should not constantly be changing.

## PROGRAM / SERVICE INCOME

Programs and services are allowed to make money and should make money. Fee-for-service, or similar mechanisms, should be part of the nonprofit's financial pie. However, program income needs to be disclosed to a grant funder. Some examples of potential program income are as follows:

- Fees earned from services provided
- Income generated from sales (needs to be declared as taxable income
- Registration or attendance fees
- Ticket sales

When grant funding helps increase program income, the income must be deducted from either the grant or any agreed-upon cost-sharing.

## CARRYFORWARD / NO COST EXTENSIONS

Many grants will span multiple years. However, the funding will be dispersed yearly. If the funds for the current year have not been used up for any reason, a carryforward will need to be requested. The funder will want to know why the funds were not used as planned and how the following year's budget will be adjusted. In most instances, this will be approved. However, if the remaining funds are too high, the funder might hold back the funding for the next year until more spend down happens. If an unspent balance remains at the end of the grant period, a no-cost extension must be requested. Again, justification will need to be filed. In this case, it asks the funder for additional time to spend down the grant. There are many reasons this can happen, such as recruitment taking longer than anticipated, staffing issues, data analysis delays, etc. Most importantly, it needs to be disclosed, justified, and appropriately requested to carry over.

## AUDITING / SITE VISITS

When it comes to post-award management, both internal and external auditing needs to take place. Internal auditing of grants should be done on a formal and informal basis. It is always best to find internal errors and correct them before an external audit finds them. Funders may request external audits randomly or if they have reason to believe there has been a misuse of funds. They rely heavily on the reports of whistleblowers. If an external audit takes place, they look at your grants randomly, and if an error is found, they will assume it is happening across the board, and fines will be charged accordingly.

## GRANT AWARD CLOSEOUT

The closeout process needs to begin at the end of the grant period. It is important to notify any employees solely employed by the grant that it is ending and termination documents will be processed. Severance will need to be paid for these individuals. Often, these individuals will be laid off before the end of the grant so the grant can absorb the severance costs; otherwise, the nonprofit is responsible for paying this.

Funders will require a complete program report and financial report at the end of the grant. Below are some of the items that will need to be completed:

- Review the terms of the award to ensure that all deliverables are submitted at the designated due dates;
- Verify that all costs charged to the project are appropriate and in line with the outcomes and/or deliverables;
- Confirm all expenses have been posted;
- Review expenditures for allowability;
- Identify and resolve all outstanding invoices (Accounts Receivable and Accounts Payable);
- Ensure all journal entries and Misc. Batches have been completed and processed;
- Verify that all encumbrances have cleared;
- Close Purchase Orders;
- Ensure Sub-recipients' final invoices have been paid;
- Account for any property or equipment purchased with grantor funds and are managed according to grantor terms for close out purposes;
- Run a Trial Balance report to verify grant revenue and expenses are in balance;
- Reconcile the General Ledger to Grants Accounting Subledger and make corrections/adjustments as necessary;
- Review fund balance to ensure grant funds are used within the allowed award amount by the grantor;
- Refund any cash balances that the grantor paid in advance or paid and that are not authorized to be retained;
- Verify all cost-sharing/match commitments have been met;
- Confirm all time and effort reports are appropriate and certified;
- Submit the final financial closeout report to the grantor (this will vary from funder to funder, so their requirements need to be reviewed);

Lastly, it is essential to adequately document all grant transactions and retain them based on the grantor's requirements.

## SUMMARY

In summary, effective program management consists of many components. First, there needs to be a timely review of grant expenditures. These need to be well documented and signed off on by all parties. There should be monthly grant meetings to review the program and financial progress. This helps to keep everyone on the same page. All communications should be timely. If something arises, it should be disclosed immediately, not waiting for an upcoming meeting. If sub-awards are involved, they need to be closely monitored. Lastly, if cost sharing or matching is applicable, timely reporting and allocation are critical. It is wise to start with the end in mind. Since day one, keep in mind what will be expected at the close out of the grant to ensure good grants management will help maintain trust and transparency with the funder, which will heighten the likelihood of future funding

# CHAPTER TWELVE
## Case Study

### GETTING GRANTED: READY OR NOT?

Heather received a call from her brother, Matt, asking her to help out a friend, Todd, the owner of Connected Living (CL). Matt told her they wanted to hire a consultant to help apply for a federal grant. Heather asked Matt about the program, but he did not know much, and she was concerned that she could not take on another client at this time. A project of this magnitude would take a minimum of 100 plus hours to complete. However, Heather agreed to a call with CL since Todd was a friend of her brother. She felt she owed him that much.

### CL/PROGRAM BACKGROUND

Connected Living is a privately held social-impact technology company. They have demonstrated success in reaching low-income seniors, people with disabilities, and mature adults residing in public and federally subsidized housing. CL has an innovative workforce, creative programming, and a developed understanding of deploying technology to these populations. They wanted to apply for a federal grant to help support one of their newer programs, "Better Outcomes for Northern Illinois Seniors."

In the "BONIS" project, Connected Living will deploy a team of "Wellness Ambassadors" to digitally enable and train a representative population of low-income seniors and people with disabilities so that they become engaged in the management of their care. Selecting two randomly digitized groups of participants, the project will demonstrate how innovative educational programming combined with simplified medical monitoring can impact reduced admissions, fewer re-admissions, and a slower transition to custodial care from four of the most expensive (and prevalent) Diagnosis-related Groups (Chronic Obstructive Pulmonary Disease, Hyper Tension, Congestive Heart Failure, Diabetes Mellitus). The potential cost savings and improved outcomes in a representative sample of Northern Illinois cities will present significant improvements and economies on how Medicare and Medicaid serve low-income populations if the program is replicated and sustained.

### THE INITIAL CALL

A few days later, Heather had a preliminary phone call with Todd. She found out that CL was planning on applying for a National Institutes of Health (NIH) grant that was due in less than 30 days. The minute Heather heard this; she instinctively thought to herself, "No way is that happening in 30 days. It takes at least 100 hours to complete a federal grant application." She commented to Todd that this was not a lot of time to write a competitive federal grant proposal.

Additionally, she voiced her concerns that she was coming in as an external partner and had a lot to learn about CL. Not to mention developing relationships and trust with the employees to gain their buy-in to help with the process. If she were even going to attempt to help with this grant, she would not be able to do it alone. Todd told her the employees were already on board and had already started writing the grant. They just needed some expert guidance. Heather told Todd she would be in touch but made no promises at the end of their call.

Heather immediately called her brother, Matt. When he answered the phone, she said, "What did you get me into?" Matt was silent. He did not know firsthand what Heather was referring to, never having written a grant. Heather continued, "They have only written one grant before, and this is a federal application due in less than 30 days. This is going to take me at least 100 hours. I have no idea how Todd expects this to get done!" Matt asked her to do him a personal favor and do her best to guide them. He also confided in Heather that he had personally invested in the company and had a stake in seeing them succeed. In the end, Heather caved and agreed to help CL, but it would be expensive.

The next day Heather called Todd and said she would help them, but she could not guarantee the results. She also told Todd that her rate was $100 per hour. Todd did not even blink an eye and agreed. Heather did have some additional requests:

- Access to any and all needed financials
- Access to all programmatic information
- A copy of the previous grant application
- Access to any and all necessary resources (including staff)

Again, Todd agreed without hesitation. Heather said they needed to start immediately, and they decided on a planning meeting at 8 am the next day. Also, could he email her a copy of what has been created to read it and see what they have to begin with? About an hour later, Heather received an email from Todd with an attached document. Heather started to read through the notes and what was already written. She thought that this was not a bad start, and that they have a well-developed outline to work with. Heather then noticed that there were some comments in the margin. As she read them, she noted that the commenter's name was Grant Writers, Ltd. She emailed Todd back, asking how this was as no one else had been mentioned. He said it was a previous company they had hired but no longer worked with them. Heather was curious about this; she asked Todd why. All he said was that they had professional differences. This left Heather feeling unsettled, but it was too late to turn back.

## THE PLANNING MEETING

As everyone came into the conference room the following day for the planning meeting, Heather sat in silence, taking in the room and the dynamics. For the most part, everyone seemed friendly but not overly assertive. Someone asked Todd how he was feeling. He said he was feeling great. Heather thought that was odd but assumed Todd must have been under the weather recently. Todd started the meeting by welcoming everyone and introducing Heather to the team. They all went around the table and made brief introductions on who they were and their role at CL. Heather jotted down some notes as she knew this would come in helpful as they moved forward and save time as she would know exactly who to go to for answers or resources. Her first impression was that this was a great group of individuals and passionate about their work. Everyone seemed happy and appeared to have great synergy with one another. Heather was impressed with the team and the people Todd had working for CL. One obvious thing was their passion for the organization's mission.

Heather did ask if anyone had any experience writing grants. She soon discovered they knew very little about grants and did not have any pre-established policies in place. This was unchartered waters for CL. As Heather was looking over the request for proposal (RFP), she saw they had missed all of the funders planning meetings. These meetings help potential applicants get questions clarified and additional guidance about the application. Heather felt like they were climbing uphill on this application and were so far behind. She made a few notes about the RFP for after the meeting:

- Email the contact person at NIH to see if there were any recordings of the planning meetings
- 3 Year Grant
- $10,000,000 Direct Cost Cap
- Indirect Costs calculated based on their Negotiated Rate
- Needs to be submitted by 11:59 pm EST, not the usual 5 pm EST
- Target population are low-income individuals suffering from one or more co-morbidities

Since this grant would be submitted through grants.gov, Heather asked Todd if they had established a signing authority and had all the proper logins. Todd assured Heather they had everything they needed. Knowing there was no time to waste, Heather did not verify this information and trusted what Todd told her. Heather asked if they had submitted their Letter of Intent and Todd said Andrew had submitted it and handed her a copy.

January 25, 2012

Mary Greene
Grants Management Officer
Office of Acquisition and Grants Management
Centers for Medicare and Medicaid Services
U.S. Department of Health and Human Services
Mail Stop B3-30-03
7500 Security Blvd, Baltimore, MD 21218

Re: Application for a Cooperative Agreement Award for the "Better Outcomes for Northern Illinois Seniors" Program

Dear Ms. Greene,

I am the Authorized Organizational Representative of Connected Living, Inc., which is applying for a Cooperative Agreement with the Center for Medicare & Medicaid Innovation of the Centers for Medicare & Medicaid Services of the U.S. Department of Health and Human Services.

The Cooperative Agreement we seek is to fund a program titled "Better Outcomes for Northern Illinois Seniors" or "BONIS" which aims to prove better outcomes at lower costs for low income seniors who reside in public and rental assistance housing in three Northern Illinois cities.

To deliver the outcomes anticipated in the project, Connected Living will team up with three public housing authorities, local EMS and hospital providers, and local governments and stakeholders. Northern Illinois University will provide evaluation to measure the effectiveness of the program.

Connected Living is requesting funding in the amount of $9,945,848 for this program.

As the principal contact person for this project, please direct any questions or requests for further information to me.

On behalf of our entire team, I look forward to the possibility of demonstrating a health care innovation with major implications for improving the delivery of care and health outcomes to the 8.7 million U.S. low income seniors receiving rental assistance from the federal government.

Sincerely yours,
Andrew Lowenstein
Chief Operating Officer

Heather was relieved to know this part was done. Knowing they had no time to waste, she told everyone she would start writing the grant right after the meeting. Anna, Bill, and Gina all said they would clear their schedules for the day and assist. Heather said that is great and if you could complete an information sheet for me that would be helpful. Having people stepping up to help made Heather feel a little better about their ability to accomplish this. She would have to beg for people to help her on other projects, and they did. They were not motivated.

A couple of hours after they started working they handed Heather the information sheet about the program.

1. Project title: BONIS
2. Specific purposes for which funds are being sought: Project funds will be used to hire, train and deploy a team of "Wellness Ambassadors," low cost, non-medical health workers who will recruit and engage project participants, helping them to learn about their chronic medical conditions, make better lifestyle choices and participate in regular medical monitoring. Project funds will also pay to digitally enable these participants with computers, Internet connections and remote monitoring devices. The project team will integrate with all major local providers, teaming up with EMS, primary care and hospital partners to create early interventions and follow up on discharge plans. Finally, project funds will pay for Northern Illinois University to create an un-blinded, randomized trial of these community-based interventions.
3. Needs addressed by the proposal: Community-based intervention program that will engage underserved populations residing in low-income and subsidized housing. These individuals are poorer and sicker than privately insured individuals and do not receive the medical care they need to maintain their health.
4. Measurable Objectives Desired:
   **Goal 1:** Demonstrate a cost saving health care delivery model that both meets the prime objectives of the U.S. Dept. of Health and Human Services (improving outcomes and decreasing costs for high-cost, high-risk patient populations) and leverages that work to address a key objective of the U.S. Dept. of Housing and Urban Development (helping recipients of government rental assistance to pursue a path to independence through better health)
   **Goal 2**: Prove that better health outcomes for low income seniors can be delivered through a cost saving combination of technology adoption training, engaging wellness curricula, simplified health tracking software, and a comprehensive remote monitoring system
   **Goal 3**: Leverage existing infrastructure and training from prior federal and state digital inclusion/broadband adoption programs for low-income populations (without supplanting

existing state, local or private funding of this infrastructure or services)

**GOAL 4**: Deliver a scalable Workforce Innovation program that mobilizes CNA trained or certified personnel as Wellness Ambassadors to provide a combination of wellness and health technology training to high-risk, high-cost patient populations

**GOAL 5**: Empower high-risk, high-cost patients to become their own healthcare advocates and partner with their providers in attaining better self-managed care

**GOAL 6**: Teach program participants about The Patient Protection and Affordable Care Act (PPACA) and the benefits it offers to those living with chronic conditions during its transition (2012 through 2014)

**GOAL 7**: Reduce hospital admissions by engaging local EMS providers to make early interventions for patients whose remote monitoring/tracking systems raise trending or acute incidence alerts

**GOAL 8**: Decrease per-patient levels of Medicare/Medicaid reimbursements for the high-risk, high-cost patient population residing in federally subsidized low-income housing primarily by reducing instances of readmission

**GOAL 9**: Monitor, actively self-evaluate, and report on the progress and impact of the BONIS program in a timely manner

**GOAL 10**: Provide a formal evaluation of the effectiveness of the BONIS program through a randomized trial administered by the School of Nursing and Health Studies at Northern Illinois University

5. Method of Achieving Objectives: N/A
6. Describe the Agency and its Qualifications to Meet This Need: NIH
7. Timing (Status, date, and/or time frame of project) [in the next page]:

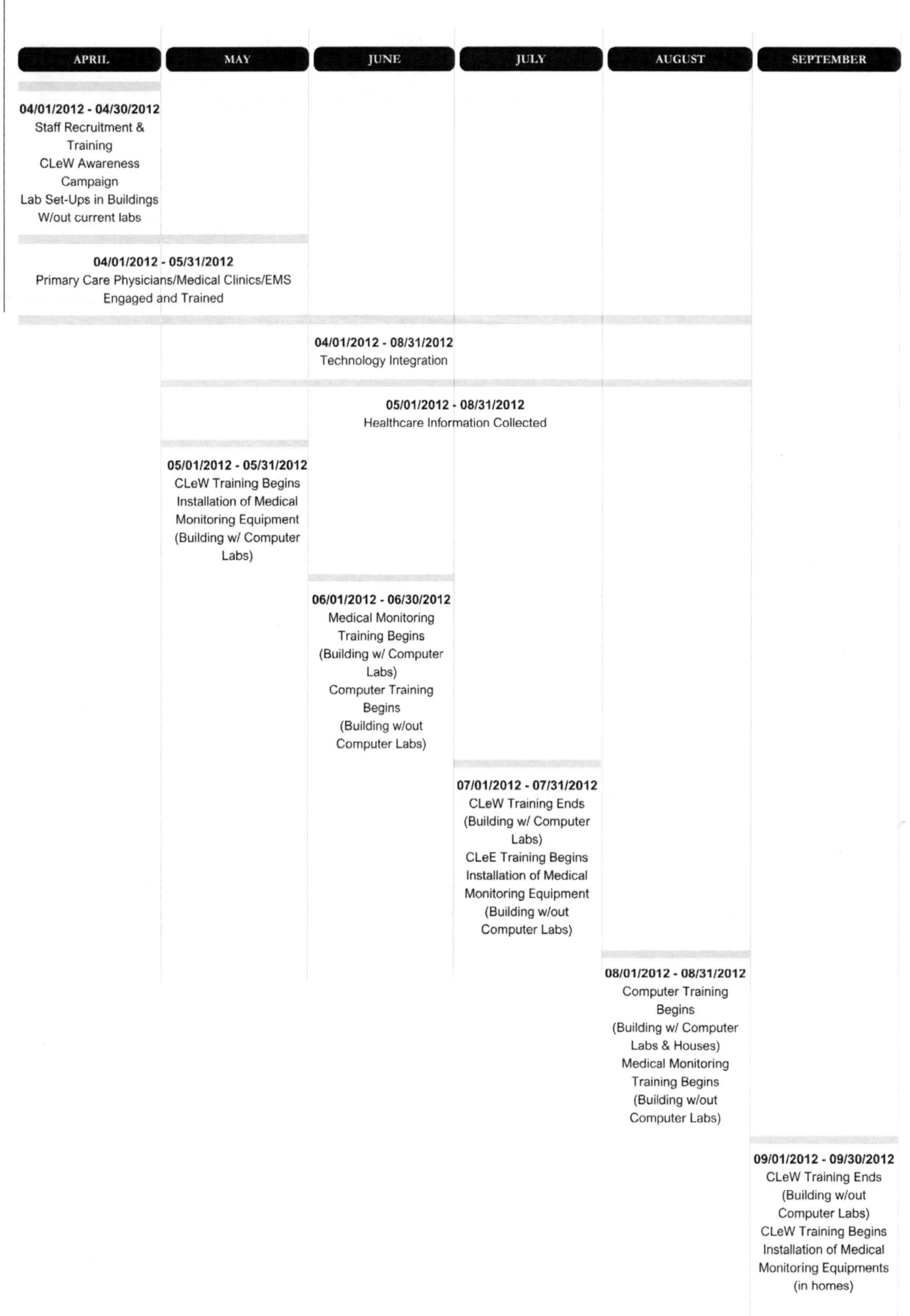
09/30/2012
End of 1st 6 Months
All Partecipants in High Rises
Or Low Rises online and receiving
Support and Monitoring
04/01/2012
BONIS Project Starts
APRIL
MAY
JUNE
JULY
AUGUST
SEPTEMBER
04/01/2012 - 04/30/2012
Staff Recruitment & Training
CLeW Awareness Campaign
Lab Set-Ups in Buildings W/out current labs
04/01/2012 - 05/31/2012
Primary Care Physicians/Medical Clinics/EMS Engaged and Trained
04/01/2012 - 08/31/2012
Technology Integration
05/01/2012 - 08/31/2012
Healthcare Information Collected
05/01/2012 - 05/31/2012
CLeW Training Begins
Installation of Medical Monitoring Equipment
(Building w/ Computer Labs)
06/01/2012 - 06/30/2012
Medical Monitoring Training Begins
(Building w/ Computer Labs)
Computer Training Begins
(Building w/out Computer Labs)
07/01/2012 - 07/31/2012
CLeW Training Ends
(Building w/ Computer Labs)
CLeE Training Begins
Installation of Medical Monitoring Equipment
(Building w/out Computer Labs)
08/01/2012 - 08/31/2012
Computer Training Begins
(Building w/ Computer Labs & Houses)
Medical Monitoring Training Begins
(Building w/out Computer Labs)
09/01/2012 - 09/30/2012
CLeW Training Ends
(Building w/out Computer Labs)
CLeW Training Begins
Installation of Medical Monitoring Equipments
(in homes)

8. How will the organization evaluate success? The evaluation will address the effects of the BONIS program on the Innovation Center's three-part aim of better health, better health care, and lower costs through improved quality.
9. Use reverse side to sketch in a project budget: Need to ask Andrew

## THE TWIST

For days on end, Heather worked with different employees from CL to get the grant written. Whenever she needed resources or questions answered, the appropriate people were available. There was no lack of resources or help. Then one day, she was working with someone new at CL, and they mentioned that there was going to be a call with a University in Chicago. Heather asked why and was told because they would be our subcontractors. She had to hold back her reaction to hearing this for the first time. Having a subcontractor added a new level of complexity. She had to ensure that CL's application aligned with theirs and that they completed and delivered their components before the deadline because she had to integrate the documents. This included a scope of work, budget, budget narrative, and biosketches.

Heather did not understand why CL was applying for the grant, and the University was the subcontractor. The application would be more competitive if the roles were reversed. The University had the history and infrastructure for managing these types of grants. CL did not have this track record. Their chances of getting funded would be heightened if the roles reversed. CL would still establish a track record managing a federal grant. This would put them in a better strategic position for the future. While she did not want to undo a lot of the work they had already done, she ethically could not sit there and not say something. Heather spoke up and asked why the University was not taking the lead on this, and they would be the subcontractors. Her question was quickly dismissed, and no one wanted to discuss this option. Heather knew if she pushed the changes making the deadline would be impossible. So she let this slide and proceeded as things were already established. Before they got off the call, they agreed on a date for them

## THE FINANCES

Heather knew that time was quickly slipping away, and she felt she needed to get started on the budget. However, she needed to see the organization's financials to complete the budget. She approached Andrew, the CFO, and asked for a copy of last year's financials, the current year's approved budget, and an income statement to date. He said no problem; he would have that to her in a day. Heather was so busy working on other aspects of the project that the financials slipped her mind, and on Friday, she realized that Andrew never got them to her. She looked for him but was told he left for the weekend but was available by email. So Heather sent him an email requesting the items again. In the email, she explained the urgency and would be working straight through the weekend. Heather checked her email all weekend, but no response from Andrew. So first thing Monday morning, she went to his office. He apologized and said she would have the documents by the end of the day. The end of the day came and went, and Heather started to feel like she was being railroaded.

She did not have any time for this political nonsense, so she emailed Todd and explained what she needed.

MON 1/12/2012 10:59 PM

TO: MCWADE, TODD
SUBJECT: FINANCIAL STATEMENTS

HI TODD,

SORRY, TO BOTHER YOU AT THIS LATE HOUR BUT I AM IN DESPERATE NEED OF CL'S FINANCIAL STATEMENTS. I HAVE TRYING TO GET COPIES FROM ANDREW SINCE FRIDAY BUT HE APPEARS TO BE HESITANT TO RELEASE THESE DOCUMENTS. COULD YOU PLEASE ASK HIM TO GIVE ME A COPY SO I CAN MOVE FORWARD WITH THE GRANT BUDGETING?

THANKS FOR YOUR ATTENTION TO THIS MATTER,
HEATHER

During lunch the next day, Andrew came and threw down a stack of paper, said I think this is what you were looking for, and walked away. His body language clearly showed that he was annoyed with Heather. She would have taken the time to address this any other time, but the clock was ticking. Heather put the documents aside to finish what she was working on. As she began to wrap up for the day, she pulled out the financials to review them. Heather immediately started seeing some red flags:

- The grant they were currently writing was being recorded as revenue
- She did not see any of her invoices being accrued under expenses
- Heather was also aware of other invoices that had been submitted recently, which were not showing up on the financial statements
- Under Donations and Pledges, there was revenue recorded based on preliminary discussions of them happening
- There diversification of income was significantly different than most nonprofits

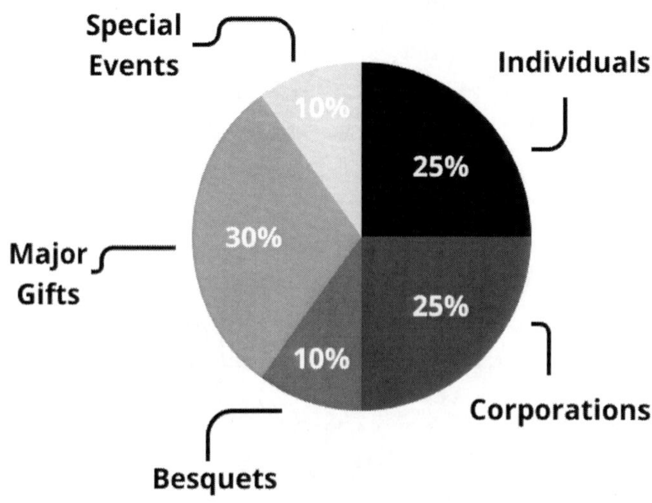

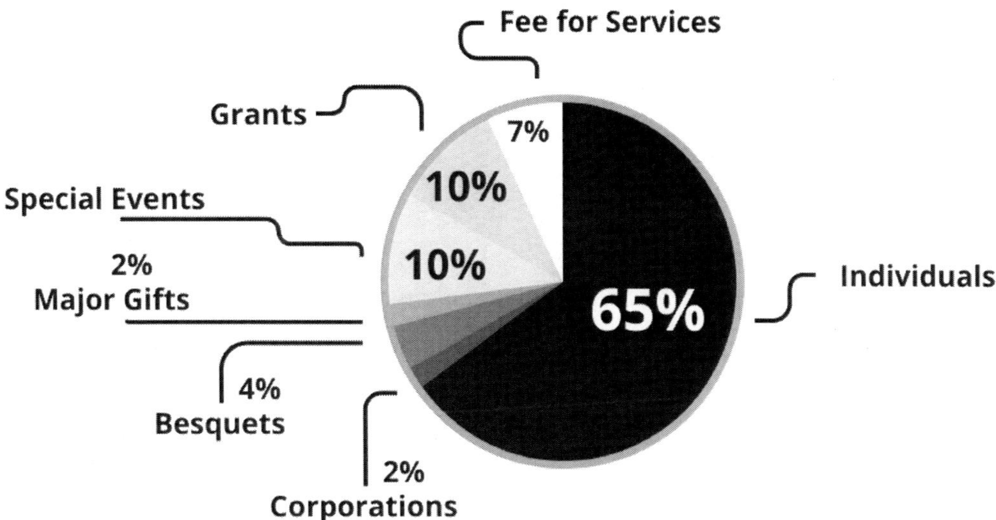


These were just a few quick things she noticed. While this made Heather uneasy, she was not hired to audit their financial documents, nor did she have the time. She decided to put this aside for the moment and stay focused on the task at hand.

She started to draft the budget. The grant was for $10,000,000 over three years. As she began assembling the budget, she needed to reach out to vendors to get quotes for submission. Heather walked down the hall to Andrew's office to find out if they had any preferred vendors they used. He gave her a list. As she reached out to the vendors on the list, she was hesitant. She quickly discovered that CL had outstanding invoices with many of the vendors. After some negotiating, she got the information she needed to complete the budget (See Appendix 1 for Budget Narrative).

## BOARD UPDATE

Todd asked Heather to have lunch with him and during this lunch he asked her for an update on the grant. Heather said it was going to be tight but she felt confident they would be able to get the grant done on time. Todd said that is great news because I have a board meeting tonight and need to provide an update. They enjoyed a nice lunch and talked about other projects and their families.

Later that night Todd arrived at the board meeting. As he entered he was one of the first to arrive. He started talking with Linda and boasting about the grant and how they were guaranteed to get the funding. Linda was surprised but happy to hear this. Slowly the remainder of the board members arrived. Charles then said well it looks like everyone is here. Should we order a round of beers before we get started? Quickly, everyone agreed. They began to work through the meeting agenda and finally got to the grant update. Todd said everything was going well and they would be meeting the deadline without any issues. He also said that as long as they got the grant submitted they were guaranteed funding. The board was elated to hear this news. They said this would help with some of the financial constraints they had been feeling recently. Todd then made a motion for a 10% pay increase which the Board unanimously approved.

## FINAL STAGES

Finally, after many hours of working and writing, they needed to begin adding in research. Heather asked for the sources to add, and she was met with blank stares. No one had any idea what she was talking about. Heather could not believe they did not have research or data to include, never mind reading a peer-reviewed journal. She asked everyone what they had based their writing on. They responded with our experiences and personal beliefs on the subject. Heather just shook her head. There was no time to get into why this was wrong. She just needed to keep moving forward. She gave them a crash course on how to search for these resources. There was no time to teach them how to analyze and code the articles, so she just set them up to search while coding and analyzing. At this point, Heather's frustration was mounting. Usually, this work would be done by a research assistant. While Heather did not feel the job was beneath her, there were just many deliverables to balance, and she did not have time to sort through all these articles. She spent the entire night in the office completing this research component because they were 48 hours away from the submission deadline.

Heather could not believe they had made it to submission day. While there was still much to be done, the light was at the end of the tunnel. As the day progressed, you could feel the bustle in the office. Files were being edited, converted to pdf, and uploaded. The budget was being finalized and uploaded. The last documents from the subcontractors were being uploaded. At 5 pm EST the files were done and ready to be submitted. While Heather likes things to be done earlier, she was relieved they had finished before the deadline. She suggested they submit the grant now, but management wanted to wait and continue editing the documents. This went on for a few hours.

At 11 pm EST, Heather began to sweat. She knew they needed to hit the submit button and finally convinced them to move forward. Heather started talking with a few of the people she had been working with over the past few weeks. After a bit, she began to feel some urgency coming from the offices, then she heard someone yell out, " Do you have her number. Moments later, she heard she was not answering. Not sure about what was happening, Heather wandered towards the offices. At this point, she heard the news they could not find the password to log in to submit the grant. They had 15 minutes left to submit the grant. She got on the phone with grants.gov to talk with technical support. As she was on the phone with them, she found out that they did not have a signing authority even if they got the password sorted out. Heather's stomach sunk to her feet. There was no way to submit the grant. As she broke the news, Todd did not want to believe it and continued to try and submit. As Heather sat on the floor, she looked up at the clock and said it was 12:01 pm. We are out of time!

The silence was deafening. No one wanted to say anything. They stayed like that for at least ½ an hour. Finally, Todd said we should all go home and meet the following day for reflection. As Heather walked to her car, she felt numb. This had never happened to her before. Somehow she felt like she failed everyone. As she got into her car, it would not start. She thought this was just the icing on the cake. Luckily, Chris was outside and saw she was having trouble. He pulled his car over to help. While they had jumper cables, neither one had any idea how to jump the car. So they turned on YouTube and looked for a video. They quickly figured it out and got Heather's car going. She thanked Chris and said she would see him in a few hours. As she drove home, she began to realize she had done everything she could to make this a successful submission. They could either dwell on what happened and let it hold them back or learn from their mistakes and implement changes.

## REFLECTION

The morning came quickly. Heather walked into the reflection meeting with only a few hours of sleep. It all still seemed so surreal. A few minutes later, Todd walked in, followed by the rest of the team. He opened the meeting with the following words:

> *I want to thank everyone for their hard work over the past few months. This was not an easy task, and your determination, motivation, and engagement are inspiring. While this did not result in the ending we had hoped it would; we will not let it define us. Let's take this moment of reflection to learn and grow stronger as we move forward.*

Todd then turned the floor over to Heather for her thoughts and comments. Heather decided this was an opportunity to help guide them and set the foundation for the future. Below are the key points she raised:

- CL does not have a strong Grants management background. Moving forward, I would recommend smaller grants or partnerships. This will strengthen CL's opportunity to get a grant funded and demonstrate to funders your ability to manage the post-award functions.
- Someone on staff should be training in grant writing and research analysis. Since I was the only one who knew how to do this, it took time away from other aspects of the grant writing process.
- CL should create a policy and procedure manual for pre-award and post-award management.

A few of the other staff members spoke about how they felt overwhelmed and in over their heads at times. They felt the need for additional training and education in the grant writing field if the company planned on continuing to do. Todd thanked everyone for coming in so early after a late night and told them to take the remainder of the day off.

As everyone stood to leave, Heather asked Todd if he had a moment to speak. He said, of course, and told her to come into his office. Heather followed him down the hall. As she sat, Todd turned to her and said I want you to know we know you did everything you could to get his grant accomplished. We appreciate the professionalism you demonstrated throughout the entire process. Heather thanked Todd for his words and said I wanted to bring something up but did not feel the meeting was appropriate. As I reviewed the financials that Andrew gave me for the grant, I saw some things that concerned me.

Again, I am not sure if this is my place to say anything, but since you are such good friends with my brother, I felt I could not keep quiet. Todd assured Heather that he wanted to hear what she had to say. Heather told him about the red flags she noticed and the conversations she had with the vendors. Todd was shocked and not aware. Heather had difficulty understanding how Todd missed this or was not aware. He clearly saw her body language and said to Heather I have not been as present as I should have been. I have a brain tumor and have been out of the office lately for treatments. Heather said I am so sorry to hear this I had no idea. Todd said there was no way for you to no, and the good thing is I just found out I am in remission. The mood immediately lightened. Todd thanked Heather again for all her help and handed her her check. As Heather walked out of CL, she felt saddened that her time was ending. She had made some great connections and friends. While they were busy during this past month, this already helped create a strong bond between her and some employees.

**Appendix 1 – Budget Narrative**

***5.1 Budget Form SF 424A and Budget Narrative* - Period of Performance: 4/1/2012-3/31/2015**

**Personnel:** Year 1: $896,583, Year 2: $1,005,709, and Year 3: $893,808. Itemized costs below:

-- Gina Baxter, (1 FTE 36 months) **Project Manager**, (Year 1: $90,000, Year 2: $92,700, and Year 3: $95,481) will manage the project team and oversee all aspects of grant implementation. Further responsibilities of this position are described in Section 2.3 above.

-- TBN (1 FTE 36 months) **Grant Administrator**, (Year 1: $75,000 Year 2: (50%) $77,250 and Year 3: (50%) $79,568) will be responsible for the distribution of all technology, for broadband enablement, and for lab and network configuration. Further responsibilities of this position are described in Section 2.3 above.

-- TBN (x2 FTE 1st 18 months; x1 FTE for last 18 months) **Health Liaison**, (Year 1: $105,417 Year 2: $84,975, and Year 3: $58,350) will serve as the interface with local provider partners, ensuring the project works seamlessly with hospitals to track participant outcomes. Further responsibilities of this position are described in Section 2.3 above.

-- TBN (x2 FTE), **Training/Operations Directors**, (Year 1: $ 105,000, Year 2: $ 123,600, and Year 3: $ 127,308) will be responsible for hiring, training, and managing FT and PT WAs. Further responsibilities of this position are described in Section 2.3 above.

-- TBN, (1 FTE 1st 24 months; x0.5 FTE for last 12 months) **Director of Technology**, (Year 1: $75,000 Year 2: $77,250 and Year 3: $39,784) will be responsible for the distribution of all technology and equipment and for lab and network configuration. Further responsibilities of this position are described in Section 2.3 above.

-- TBN, (x0.5 FTE 1st 18 months) **IT Support Specialist**, (Year 1: $30,000 Year 2: $15,450, and Year 3: $0). This position provides support to the Director of Technology. Further responsibilities of this position are described in Section 2.3 above.

-- TBN, (x0.5 FTE for 24 months) **Data Entry Specialist**, (Year 1: $25,000 Year 2: $25,000, and Year 3: $0) This position supports the proper flow of data to provider partners. Further responsibilities of this position are described in Section 2.3 above.

-- TBN (increasing to x10 FTE by month 3, and x12 FTE by month 10), **full time Wellness Ambassador**, (Year 1: $342,000 Year 2: $407,880 and Year 3: $305,539) will have CNA certification and be responsible for enrolling, training and assisting project participants, coordinating with building staff, project personnel, project partners, and technology resources to attain project goals. Further responsibilities of this position are described in Section 2.3 above.

-- TBN (x5.5 FTE), **part time Wellness Ambassador**, (Year 1: $49,167, Year 2: $126,604, and Year 3: $187,779) will be responsible for training project participants on the CLN, monitoring the computer lab, making home visits, and providing support for residents regarding laptops and internet concerns. Further responsibilities of this position are described in Section 2.3 above.

**Fringe Benefits:** Year 1: $140,455, Year 2: $166,661, and Year 3: $152,790

-- The fringe benefit rate is average to 13.2% and is comprised of health insurance and dental insurance for all full-time individuals, and payroll taxes for all employees.

**Travel:** Year 1: $54,800, Year 2: $62,200 and Year 3: $56,400. This amount includes a car allowance of $200 per staff member to travel between Rockford, DeKalb and Freeport IL, and also includes travel costs to six CMS Conferences for three project or Applicant staff members, including hotel and airfare, at the cost of $1,200 per individual per trip.

**Equipment:** No equipment costs

**Supplies:** Year 1: $525,648, Year 2: $94,618, and Year 3: $41,790. Itemized costs below:

<u>Laptop Computers for Participants</u>: Year 1: $242,562, Year 2: $36,852, and Year 3: $7,470 CL will deploy 728 of the robust HP ProBook 6565b to program participants. This laptop features durable construction, a 15.6" display, Windows 7 Home Premium, an AMD Dual-Core processor, 4GB of memory, a large 320GB high-speed hard drive, an integrated HD webcam and built-in wireless and Bluetooth connectivity. HP has made an exclusive offer to Connected Living for this laptop over $600 below web pricing.

<u>Remote Medical Monitoring Gateways</u>: Year 1: $78,975, Year 2: $12,350, and Year 3: $2,275. CL plans to deploy 288 CardiaHealth Home Gateway devices that transmit readings from medical monitors to PCs or cellular networks for Group B program participants.

<u>Remote Medical Monitoring Devices</u>: Year 1: $166,974, Year 2: $45,416, and Year 3: $32,045.

These items are CardiaHealth branded CHF Devices, COPD Devices, DM2 Devices, and HTN Devices for home monitoring. A detailed breakdown of the cost of these items can be found in Appendix I of the Supplemental Materials.

**Contractual:** Year 1: $565,417, Year 2: $499,201, and Year 3: $494,531. Itemized costs below:

Project evaluation by Northern Illinois University, Year 1: $211,417, Year 2: $220,101, and Year 3: $232,231. These figures represent the direct costs of NIU in their proposed evaluation of the program which are broken down in Appendix J of the Supplemental Materials

a baseline diagnosis testing (applicable at a rate of $125/hour), hospital and EMS Data Entry.

Baseline Diagnosis Testing: Year 1: $98,000, Year 2: $23,100, and Year 3: $6,300. These items represent third party testing from Quest Diagnostics for 718 program participants (Group A and Group B) to establish baseline diagnoses.

Hospital Data Entry Contracts: Year 1: $160,000, Year 2: $160,000, and Year 3: $160,000. This item represents annual contracts worth $32,000 with each of five local hospital partners to reimburse for 50% of a data entry specialist.

EMS Data Entry Contracts: Year 1: $96,000, Year 2: $96,000, and Year 3: $96,000. This item represents annual contracts worth $32,000 with each of three local EMS partners to reimburse for 50% of a data entry specialist.

**Construction:** No costs.

**Other Expenses:** Year 1: $571,072, Year 2: $432,682, and Year 3: $383,005 will include the costs of software integration and connectivity for participant laptops, monitoring equipment, rent for the CLeW wellness center, and CLN Community Subscriptions.

Software Integration: Year 1: $390,000, Year 2: $144,000, and Year 3: $144,000. This funding goes to third parties to create and program integration for the CLN with remote monitoring software, hospital systems and PHRs utilizing Web Services and HL7.

Connectivity for Project Participant Laptops: Year 1: $115,341, Year 2: $192,958, and Year 3: $157,213. Verizon Wireless 4G LTE (via USB modems for the ProBook laptop) at $63.83 per connection per month. Verizon's 4G LTE network provides reduced latency for faster uploads and downloads. Verizon wireless prepared special incentives for this project, including no cost on the USB modem, application of a 15% monthly discount (per line) on mobile broadband service and a $100 credit per activated line.

CardiaHealth Software License for Monitoring Devices: Year 1: $44,312, Year 2: $74,304, and Year 3: $60,372. This item represents a software license of $21.50 per month to CardiHealth to provide service for each user / disease state.

Connected Living Network (CLN) software licenses: Year 1: $21,420, Year 2: $21,420, and Year 3: $21,420. This item covers CLN license for each of the PHAs at the standard rate of $595 per community per month.

**TOTAL DIRECT CHARGES:** Year 1: $2,753,975, Year 2: $2,261,071, and Year 3: $2,022,325.

**Indirect Charges:** Year 1: $1,131,518, Year 2: $933,196, and Year 3: $843,764

Connected Living is applying to US OMB for an Indirect Rate of 38.7%, and intends to charge this rate on all modified direct charges (no indirect charges on equipment or on direct contracts after first $25,000). NIU maintains an Indirect Rate of 47.0% Individual Indirect charges for Connected Living, Inc. are for Year 1: $1,040,094 Year 2: $838,483, and Year 3: $744,224

Individual Indirect charges for Northern Illinois University are for Year 1: $91,425, Year 2: $94,712, and Year 3: $99,540

**TOTAL ELIGIBLE PROJECT COSTS:** Year 1: $3,885,493, Year 2: $3,194,266 and Year 3: $2,866,089

# APPENDIX I: Summary: Qualitative Research Methods Selected Designs

The data collection process of qualitative research traditions can take many months, a year, or even longer. The researcher needs to be well-grounded in the literature and be free to explore mixed methods to gain further insights into the phenomena being studied.

## PHENOMENOLOGICAL RESEARCH

**PURPOSE:**

Phenomenological research attempts to study a phenomenon as it appears to the researcher for the purpose of describing a phenomenon of personal, natural, and social significance. A method of investigation used to describe the different ways in which people conceptualize the world around them and examine individuals' thinking. Researchers create the data to be analyzed. This research tradition serves as a preliminary exploration or pilot work for a quantitative research design.

**DATA ANALYSIS:**

Interview data is broken into segments, as the researcher looks for themes and meanings. The textural and structural descriptions are validated and triangulated with other findings and participants.

**PARTICIPANTS**

The essential criterion is that participants have experienced the phenomenon. The number of participants in a phenomenological study may be as many as 25 participants or more.

**EXAMPLE(S):**

Interviews; Carol Gilligan explored the how conscious reality appeared to women (Gilligan, 1983).

**CORRELATIONAL**

## ETHNOGRAPHIC RESEARCH

**PURPOSE:**

Ethnographic research attempts to study cultural patterns and human behaviors of a group of people in a natural setting. Researchers create data to analyze and focus on the social structures, values, customs, rituals, and beliefs that are transmitted from generation to generation. The final research study will enable readers to understand the culture even though they may not have experienced it. This research tradition is used to predict and explain the behavior of other members of the culture.

**DATA ANALYSIS:**

Interview data is broken into segments, as the researcher looks for themes and meanings. The textural and structural descriptions are validated and triangulated with other findings and participants. Data analysis can focus on norms of social behavior, sequences of events in folktales, and accounts of stories and anecdotes using detailed descriptions.

**PARTICIPANTS**

The essential criterion is that participants are members of the culture under study. The number of participants in an ethnographic study may be as many as 25 participants or more.

**EXAMPLE(S):**

Researchers use a full range of qualitative data collection techniques such as interviews, observations, records of conversations, descriptions, time and motion data, drawings, and letters. Margaret Mead described the process of growing up in Manus society (Mead, 2001).

## HISTORICAL RESEARCH

**PURPOSE:**

Historical research attempts to discover data through a search of official documents, diaries, relics, and historical accounts of events that occurred prior to the researcher's decision to study them. The researcher searches for data to analyze. Historical research constructs reality. Historical research provides a framework for understanding the present, informing the way we make judgments, supporting reform issues, and evaluating future scenarios.

**DATA ANALYSIS:**

Data is interpreted, explained, and described in traditional historical research. Quantitative data and statistical methods of data analysis can be used to make well-grounded generalizations in quantitative historical research.

**PARTICIPANTS**

The essential criterion is the size of the data set and the extensive search for primary and secondary sources.

**EXAMPLE(S):**

Interviews, official documents, diaries, relics, settings, events, objects, correspondence, and written records. Philip Nash traced the history of the Jupiters and explored the reasons the United States offered these nuclear missiles to its European allies (Nash, 1997).

## GROUNDED THEORY RESEARCH

**PURPOSE:**

Grounded theory research attempts to study an observed phenomenon as it appears to the researcher for the purpose of interpreting the perceptions people have about a phenomenon. A method of investigation is used to describe the different ways in which people conceptualize the phenomena. The researcher creates data to analyze. This research tradition serves as a preliminary exploration for the purpose of generating a theory.

**DATA ANALYSIS:**

The interview data reveal the core categories and central ideas as an accumulation of meaning emerges from the data. Interview data is analyzed through open coding, selective coding, and memos and is analyzed for the purpose of revealing or discovering the emergent core categories.

**PARTICIPANTS**

The essential criterion is that participants are willing to explore their perceptions about the phenomenon being studied. The number of participants in a grounded theory research study may be as many as 25 participants or more, or until saturation is determined and achieved through two possible approaches: (a) a heuristic code that illuminates the interaction of language, and/or (b) numerical incidents that are determined from the data.

**EXAMPLE(S):**

Interviews.

## Summary: Quantitative Research Methods Selected Designs

### DESCRIPTIVE

**PURPOSE:**

Descriptive research is a systematic, factual description of a situation or area or interest and is used to gather facts for testing theories and hypotheses using representative samples of populations. This research's goals are to compare, identify, and evaluate.

**STATISTICS:**

Relative incidence, distribution, interrelations of variables.

Mean

Mode

Median

Range

Minimum

Maximum

Count

Standard Deviation

Standard Error

Chi-Square

F statistic

Non-parametric tests

Mann-Whitney test (Wilcoxon test)

**EXAMPLE(S):**

Surveys, census studies, questionnaire and interview studies, surveys of the literature, analyses of tests.

**RELATED TERMS:**

Sampling

Policy-oriented

Random sampling

Stratified sample

Frequency analysis

Cross breaks (cross tabulations) – e.g., 3x4, 2x2

Chi-Square Test of Independence

Observed, expected and residual values

Measures of Association

Nominal Measures (Phi-coefficient, coefficient of contingency, Cramer's V)

## CORRELATIONAL

**PURPOSE:**

Correlational research attempts to investigate the extent to which variations in one factor correspond with variations in one or more other factors (variables) based on correlation coefficients.

**STATISTICS:**

Pearson r

Multiple correlation – R2

Partial correlation

Part correlation

Canonical correlation

**EXAMPLE(S):**

To study relationship between cancer and smoking, SES and high-school drop-out rates, age and insurance rates.

**RELATED TERMS:**

B, Beta, (standardized regression coefficient), slope, intercept

Goodness of fit

Coefficient of determination (R2)

Degrees of freedom

Regression equation

Residual

Building a model

Stepwise regression

Forward selection

Backward selection

Forced entry

Histograms

Correlation versus causation

## CASUAL-COMPARATIVE OR "EX POST FACTO"

**PURPOSE:**

Causal-comparative research attempts to explore possible cause-and-effect relationships by observing some existing consequence and searching for plausible casual factors among the data.

**STATISTICS:**

See above.

**EXAMPLE(S):**

Studying reports of traffic fatalities to discover the possible effect of changes in speed limit on a major freeway.

## DEVELOPMENTAL-TIME SERIES

**PURPOSE:**

Developmental-time series research attempts to investigate patterns of change as a function of time.

Longitudinal analysis

Cross-sectional

Trend study

**STATISTICS:**

R2

F statistic

See next page

**EXAMPLE(S):** The study of research universities' finance over a decade; a cross-sectional study investigating changing attitudes toward math by sampling groups of students at ten different age levels; a trend study forecasting future growth in a university from past trends and recent application/enrollment data.

**RELATED TERMS:**

Regression line

Multicollinearity

Bivariate versus multivariate

Missing observations

## TRUE EXPERIMENTAL

**PURPOSE:** True experimental research attempts to study possible cause-and-effect relationships by exposing experimental group(s) to treatment condition(s) and comparing the results to control group(s) not receiving the treatment(s). Random assignment to groups is imperative to establish the equivalence of groups.

**STATISTICS:** See above.

**EXAMPLE(S):** An investigation of the effects of an intervention program on the attitudes of 16-year-olds to drugs and alcohol, using experimental and control groups. Use a random selection of subjects, random assignment of subjects to groups, random assignment of experimental treatments to groups, and use a pretest-posttest design which controls for the effect of pre-testing by having only one-half of the students randomly receive the pre-test.

**RELATED TERMS:**

Randomization

Control/manipulation of variables

Experimental treatment

Research hypotheses

Error or random variance

Errors of measurement

Random assignment of subjects to groups

Baseline data

Nonexperimental variables

Contamination

Tests of significance

Bias

Validity

Reliability

Instrument construction

Null hypothesis/alternate hypothesis

Directional hypothesis

Independent (input), dependent (output), and control (classificatory) variables

## QUASI-EXPERIMENTAL

**PURPOSE:**

Given a setting that does not permit control and/or manipulation of all relevant variables, the purpose of quasi-experimental research is to approximate the conditions of the true experiment.

**STATISTICS:**

See above.

**EXAMPLE(S):**

Studies of drug therapy for AIDS, where control and manipulation are not always feasible.

## APPENDIX II: Sample Grant Budget Template

| **Budget Template** | | | | | | | | | | |
|---|---|---|---|---|---|---|---|---|---|---|
| **Name** | **Role on Project** | **Persons Month** | **Base Salary Year One** | **Base Salary Year Two** | **Base Salary Year Three** | **Base Salary Year Four** | **Year One** | **Year Two** | **Year Three** | **Year Four** |
| | | | | 0 | 0 | 0 | 0 | 0 | 0 | 0 |
| | | | | | | | 0 | 0 | 0 | 0 |
| *Sub Total Salary* | | | | | | | 0 | 0 | 0 | 0 |
| **Fringe Benefits** | 0% | | | | | | | | | |
| Sub Total Personnel | | | | | | | **0** | **0** | **0** | **0** |
| **Supplies** | | | | | | | | | | |
| *Sub Total Supplies* | | | | | | | | | | |
| **Travel** | | | | | | | | | | |
| *Sub Total Travel* | | | | | | | | | | |
| **Consultants** | | | | | | | | | | |
| *Sub Total Consultants* | | | | | | | | | | |
| **Other Expenses** | | | | | | | | | | |
| *Sub Total Other Expenses* | | | | | | | | | | |
| **Total Direct Cost** | | | | | | | 0 | 0 | 0 | 0 |
| **Modified Total Direct Cost** | | | | | | | | | | |
| **Total Indirect Costs** | 0% | | | | | | 0 | 0 | 0 | 0 |
| **Total Budget** | | | | | | | **0** | **0** | **0** | **0** |

## APPENDIX III: Frequently Asked Questions

1. **Many grant funders do not like to fund the same organization two granting cycles in a row. Why is that?**
   Due to demand, organizations like to diversify their funding and allow for more opportunities for all applicants. In addition, previous organizations that received funding should have a good sustainability plan in place and not need continued funding. However, a nonprofit organization can apply again for a different program or service if it continues to meet the goals of the funder.

2. **Do all grant budgets need to include fringe benefits? For instance, it seems odd to add their benefits as there are no new employees, and the individuals working on this initiative are already full-time staff.**
   If there are full-time employees of the nonprofit working on the grant and drawing a salary from the grant, then fringe benefits will always be included. A nonprofit can allow employees to work on the grant but not charge any of their salaries to the grant. This would be listed as an in-kind donation to the grant. However, this is typically not the case. Most nonprofits apply for grants to leverage the costs of running a program or service. If an employee's salary or percentage of their salary will be charged to the grant, then the appropriate fringe benefit must also be charged. For example, if ten percent of their salary is allocated to the grant budget, then only fringe benefits for that ten percent will be added to the budget.

3. **How should newer nonprofit organizations approach searching for grants? Should they only look at foundations vs. government funding? Should they wait a few years before applying for any grants? Are there any particular tips for starting out?**
   Start-up nonprofits should wait to apply for grants until they have collected some data on their programs and/or services to demonstrate their program and/or service's impact on their identified population. When starting, nonprofits must also show they have the infrastructure and experience to manage a grant. One good technique is to partner with another organization that can apply for the grant and subcontracts a portion to your new nonprofit organization. This will allow you to build a positive reputation in the grant world; as for the type of funder, you always want to start small and build up from there. Based on that, you will likely begin with foundations and progress from there. Few foundations will consider funding pilot programs, which could be an option early on, but they are few and far between.

4. **How should one approach contacting/calling the sponsor of a grant? What ways to initiate a conversation with them and increase your chances of being funded?**
   Federal and state sponsors will typically offer webinars or meetings for their RFP's. Someone from your organization will need to attend this and develop a positive relationship with the funders. For foundations, you may or may not have this initial meeting. If you do not, the RFP should list a contact person. I would begin by emailing them but be mindful of their time. Also, you want to reach out to your Board of Directors to see if they have any connections or know someone that does. These types of introductions are always the best.

5. **Where can I find samples of past proposals that were funded? Is this something I can search for using The Foundation Center Directory?**
   General searches on the Internet will help with this. However, you have to remember that many

grant applications contain confidential and, at times, proprietary information, so they will not be made public. You might be able to look at sample applications directly on the funder's site. When you are new to grant writing, hiring a consultant for training is the best way to learn how to write a grant.

6. **What should a nonprofit do before hiring a grant writer?**
   Nonprofit organizations should spend much time thinking through the project before hiring a grant writer. They should answer questions, such as, Who will this project serve? What are our goals? How will it be managed?" Organization should not just ask for money for general operational costs, but rather for a specific project to meet a particular need. After this, the grant writer can put their footprint on the project, add ideas, and help it develop into a full proposal.

7. **How much do we need to pay to hire a grant writer?**
   The amount you pay for a grant writer will vary based on their experience. Some consultants will charge per-hour rates, while others will charge based on the project. This is a negotiation process between the organization and the consultant. You must be prepared to pay your grant writer even if your organization does not get the grant. Payment doesn't necessarily need to be paid upfront, but a contract for compensation needs to be secured before they start writing. The price could be half up front, half after grant submission, whatever works for the organization and grant writer.

8. **Can I use the same proposal as last year and update a few details?**
   Absolutely not! Doing a copy-and-paste version of last year's submission would severely hinder you from being taken seriously by the funder. It would not demonstrate organizational growth from the previous submission. A funding agency will change its RFP to catch those organizations too lazy to update their old proposal. Always ensure your proposal is newly written, even if you use data or program descriptions from previous grant submissions.

9. **What are the four main areas program budgets should focus on**
   #1. PERSONNEL SERVICES - project staff expenses and the % of their time
   #2: FRINGE BENEFITS - SS tax, health insurance, vacation, sick pay, etc.
   #3: OTHER THAN PERSONNEL SERVICES - all costs associated with the project that are not staffing costs
   #4: INDIRECT COSTS - overhead or administrative costs that cannot be reflected in the program budget but are required to keep doors open

10. **How long should a cover letter be? What should it consist of?**
    It should be BRIEF- no more than half to 1 page. 1-2 sentences statement of the request and 1-2 reasons why you apply to this particular foundation.

11. **What kind of writing style is most effective?**
    A direct and clear writing style should be used in writing a grant. Use headings and bulleted lists to help the reader find important information. Avoid the usage of wordy explanations or an academic writing style. Your focus should be on the positive impact your project has.

12. **What is the difference between Goals and Objectives?**
The goal describes the general impact you hope to have on the problem you have defined without necessarily indicating the magnitude; Objectives are measurable steps toward your ultimate goals. Objectives are specific and should include the following information:

    1. Who is affected?
    2. How much is that group affected in measurable terms?
    3. During what time period the effect of the change will occur?

13. **Most foundations and corporations request some of the same standard attachments; these attachments include:**
501(c)3 form; Recent financial statement, List of key officers, board members; Organization's budget; 990 forms and the latest Annual report.

14. **Can Volunteer Services programs seek funding via grants?**
Many foundations have a history of supporting volunteerism, including the Kellogg Foundation, UPS Foundation, and TimeWarner. Also, grant writers can add support requests in grants written for programming not explicitly considered volunteer services.

15. **What is the difference between a private foundation and a public charity?**
Private Foundation: derives the majority of funds from one source- an individual, family, or corporation;
Public Charity: Receives its funds from many sources and must continue to raise funds from a variety of sources to keep its public status.

16. **How do foundations base their yearly giving?**
Foundations base their yearly giving on an average of assets from previous years.

17. **What are the most common grant writing mistakes?**
    - Not following instructions
    - Failing to research the funders' interests thoroughly. Make sure that the grant aligns itself with your needs.
    - Focusing the proposal on the needs of your organization
    - Preaching to the choir. Never assume the funder knows anything about your organization, especially when describing your capacity to carry out the project for which you seek funding. And while you're at it, avoid catchphrases and jargon. Clear, simple language wins the day.
    - Not asking for the money. You wouldn't believe how many people forget to include the grant amount they seek in the proposal. The people at the foundation aren't mind readers! Be explicit about how much you would like them to give you, usually in the first sentence or two.
    - Asking for the wrong amount. In your research, you should determine what size grants the funder has made to similar organizations. When you look at their grants list, you'll see that most funders have a number they seem fond of. Asking for substantially less or more than their typical grant will fail.

- Submitting sloppy budgets. The budget accompanying a grant proposal should be prepared with the same care as the narrative description and match it point by point.
- Submitting a proposal late. This is the most amateurish and easily avoided mistake, yet it always happens.
- Skipping the review

18. **Where should a small nonprofit look first for grants?**
If your nonprofit has never applied for a grant or doesn't have a large number of donors, then local funding is the best place to start. You must build credibility for your organization and a group of supporters who will vouch for your success. Relationships are among the most significant and often overlooked factors in winning foundation funding. You need to build those first. After receiving support locally, you can move to regional and national funders.

19. **Where can I find international grants?**
Here are some sources for researching international grants:

- Foundation Center
- USAID
- Society of Research Administrators (SRA) International website
- NonProfitExpert.com International Grants
- A comprehensive list is available at King County Library System's Nonprofit and Philanthropy Resource Center. Select the "International" tab for a variety of resources.

20. **How important is the evaluation component of the grant application?**
Grantmakers do want to know how the program **<u>will</u>** create positive results. Even when the program was not as successful as projected, it is okay to state its failure because honesty shows that the grantee would likely utilize what did not work to improve and eventually get the desired results. If this is omitted from the grant application, it could be grounds for the grant not being funded.

21. **Can a grantee, after being rejected, re-apply for that same grant the following year or the next deadline?**
It depends on the funder and their rules. Most federal applicants will not be funded on their first attempt and must resubmit. The grantee should find out why they did not receive a grant and how they could improve a future application. The grantee should use the feedback to increase the chance of getting funded with the following application.

22. **If the award is less than the costs of what it would take to run the program over a length of time, would grantors be less inclined to support such a program? Or would it depend on the size of the gap?**
As long as the grantee shows where the additional funds would come from, the funder has no issue awarding the grant requested. However, granting money to a program that would fail due to a lack of support or funding is not ideal. The grantee must strongly prove how they will receive the additional funds. It is typical to see this funding as a cost share from the nonprofit organization. Nonprofits should form a policy around this because this could cause more of a financial burden than is necessary.

23. **How do you make your proposal more exciting and engaging?**
One way is to include quotations and stories from clients, staff, volunteers, etc. They must be appropriate in content and length to adhere to word limits. Also, balance this qualitative data with quantitative data to demonstrate impact.

24. **When a grant requires matching funds, what counts towards the match?**
It depends on the funder. Check with them directly, but contributions from individuals and businesses are universally accepted. It is a good idea to connect with local businesses beforehand and inform them about the grant to build a relationship. Sometimes a nonprofit's cash reserves can count towards the matching funds. Some organizations will accept in-kind donations towards the match, which can include donated materials, staff or volunteer time, pro bono work with an ad agency, donated space, use of equipment, software, mailings, etc., as long as it is well-documented and tracked.

25. **How will the grant funder monitor the use of their grant after delivering it?**
It will depend on the funder. They will tell you up front when you apply. If it is used for donation, there will likely be no reporting. An actual grant will have a report which is due. This report is scheduled for federal grants at the end of the year and at the end of the grant itself. Most federal grants span 2-5 years. The same is usually true for state-funded awards. Foundations will all have their standards. However, since these usually only go for one year, they most likely will want a report at the end of the year. Yet, I have also seen requests for quarterly and mid-year reporting.

26. **What is a reasonable amount for a nonprofit organization to spend on its overhead or indirect cost? Is there an actual percentage number to use as a reference?**
There is no set answer for this. Every organization is different in size and need. You do want to keep it as low as possible, but what is reasonable is unique to every organization. Many people say it should be 70/30 or 80/20. This may or may not be suitable. Each organization need to be addressedseparately. In terms of the indirect cost, this will be governed by the funder. Foundations can range from zero to 15%. This will be negotiated for federal grants and will differ between on-campus and off-campus activities.

27. **In terms of sustainability, is it reasonable to tell a grantor that you will be able to fundraise to cover the grant's cost after it expires?**
Yes and no! This is not much different than saying we would look for another grant. However, fundraising is a big part of a nonprofit. So it is fair to mention this and discuss projected revenue from these events. You would want to ensure you have another revenue stream mentioned. Diversity in our revenue sources is essential for long-term sustainability.

28. **If a group of people just recently created a nonprofit organization (NPO), is it reasonable for the NPO to *immediately hit the streets* - without starting any other type of fundraising - and try to get community grant money from corporations like Walmart, Target, Stop & Shop, and Home Depot, to start setting up operations and services for the NPO? Then, after the applications are in, start planning a fundraising event to establish income sources.**
I usually advise nonprofits not to begin with grants. To get an actual grant you need to prove your program is valid and reliable. A few funders might consider a pilot program. Fundraising is a better

way to start. On the other hand, some of the items you mention to get funded could be a grant. There are grants out there that are not true grants but rather, as I like to call them, 'applied for donations'. These are for items that do not require reporting. You could look for something along those lines

Made in United States
North Haven, CT
25 September 2023